# Haunted Nashville

## Frankie Harris and Kim Meredith Harris

Schiffer Publishing Ltd

4880 Lower Valley Road, Atglen, Pennsylvania 19310

**Other Schiffer Books on Related Subjects**
**Tennessee Ghosts,**
978-0-7643-3118-3, $14.99
**Memories of Memphis,**
1-7643-2288-5, $19.95

Designed by Stephanie Daugherty
Type set in Badloc ICG/NewBskvllBT
ISBN: 978-0-7643-3120-6
Printed in China

Schiffer Books are available at special
discounts for bulk purchases for sales
promotions or premiums. Special editions,
including personalized covers, corporate
imprints, and excerpts can be created in
large quantities for special needs. For more
information contact the publisher:

Published by Schiffer Publishing Ltd.
4880 Lower Valley Road
Atglen, PA 19310
Phone: (610) 593-1777
Fax: (610) 593-2002

E-mail:
Info@schifferbooks.
com

For the largest selection
of fine reference books
on this and related
subjects, please visit our
web site at:
**www.schifferbooks.com**
We are always looking for
people to write books on
new and related subjects.
If you have an idea for a
book please contact us at
the above address.

This book may be
purchased from the
publisher.Include $5.00
for shipping. Please
try your bookstore
first. You may
write for a free
catalog.

In Europe, Schiffer
books are distributed by
Bushwood Books
6 Marksbury Ave.
Kew Gardens
Surrey TW9 4JF England
Phone: 44 (0) 20 8392-8585;
Fax: 44 (0) 20 8392-9876
E-mail: info@bushwoodbooks.co.uk
Website: www.bushwoodbooks.co.uk
Free postage in the U.K., Europe;
air mail at cost.

# Dedication

*For Logan and Cole —*
*The motivation for everything we do.*

# Acknowledgements

e would like to thank the following people for their help with this project:

Amber Vinson, for taking some of the wonderful pictures used in this book; Beth Handel and Amy Dunlap, for the helpful critique and editing of the earliest drafts; Molly Altenbern, for the headshots used on the "About the Authors" page; James Q. Meredith, for all his assistance and knowledge of historic weaponry; Shirley Meredith, for all her help and support; Woody Harris, for his enthusiasm and faith in our various projects; and Frances Harris, who would have loved this book.

Also, thanks to the countless eyewitnesses who have so graciously shared their stories with us; Past Perfect, Mulligan's, Buffalo Billiard's and Tootsie's Orchid Lounge for allowing us to bring ghost tours into your establishments and the great service over the years; all of the talented tour guides, who have so successfully brought their gifts of drama and passion to the stories; the Nashville Public Library for all of their help in gathering research; and, finally, to our editor Dinah Roseberry and everyone at Schiffer Publishing for this amazing opportunity.

# Contents

Foreword ............................................................................. 6

Chapter One: Old Hickory Rides Again ................................ 8

Chapter Two: The State Capitol ......................................... 17
*Fighting Spirits • Forever on Guard • Polk's Tomb • Rachel in the Tower*

Chapter Three: The Hermitage Hotel .................................. 29
*Room 910 • The Lady in White • The Southern Belle*

Chapter Four: The Lost Tomb of St. Mary of the Seven Sorrows ........ 39

Chapter Five: Lady at the Top of the Stairs ........................ 50

Chapter Six: Ghosts of the Ryman Auditorium ..................... 53

Chapter Seven: Tootsie's Orchid Lounge ............................. 66

Chapter Eight: Poltergeists ............................................... 70

Chapter Nine: Adelicia Acklen ......................................... 77

Chapter Ten: Death to Free Speech .................................... 91

Chapter Eleven: The Haunted Tavern ................................. 97

Chapter Twelve: Living in the Past .................................... 102

Chapter Thirteen: Last Stop at Union Station ..................... 119

Chapter Fourteen: Murder in Printer's Alley ...................... 128

Chapter Fifteen: The Savage House ................................... 137

Chapter Sixteen: The Tragedy of Georgia and Charlie .......... 142

Chapter Seventeen: The Morgue ....................................... 145

Chapter Eighteen: Hume-Fogg .......................................... 148
*Sibling Rivalry*

Chapter Nineteen: Past Perfect ......................................... 152

Chapter Twenty: Curse of the Bell Witch ........................... 158

Bibliography ................................................................... 173

Index ............................................................................. 175

# Foreword

O ur interest in ghost stories is one of the things we had in common before we were married. On vacations we inevitably would take the local ghost tour or pick up a book on local hauntings. Curious about our own city's haunted history, we began doing research in our spare time. We were surprised to discover that Nashville had an amazing collection of ghostly accounts. Many of the best stories involved the magnificent historic buildings in the downtown area. Together we created a route and opened Nashville Ghost Tours. It took patience, but what started out as a seasonal tour open only the six weeks around Halloween has grown into a year-round business. The interest in Nashville's hauntings continues to grow.

The idea of including all of these stories into a single book had been recommended over the years. The book in your hands is a compilation of the ghost stories of the city of Nashville. Each story is an attempt to take the many sources and pieces of information and combine them into a cohesive and entertaining story. Some liberties have been taken where necessary for dramatic effect, but the historic facts and the stories themselves have not been fictionalized. It's our hope that the following chapters do not read as a simple laundry list of haunted buildings, but as compelling dramatic scenes giving the reader the feel of being in the moment of these often terrifying occurrences. All of the stories take place in Nashville with the exception of one: the Bell Witch. Although the Bell Witch ghost story took place in Adams, Tennessee, just a forty-five minute drive north of downtown, it seemed appropriate to include it here for a couple of reasons. One is that it's the area's most famous ghost story, and the Bell Witch is known throughout the world. The other reason is that there is a connection between Nashville and the Bell Witch. Many of the witnesses and descendents of the Bell family lived in Nashville. Those ghost stories are part of the fabric of Nashville's culture.

We hope that you will find these ghost stories as fascinating as we did.

## About Nashville Ghost Tours

Many of the sites in this book are included in the routes offered by Nashville Ghost Tours. A lantern-bearing guide dressed in period costume leads the Haunted Downtown Tour. Guests have often captured ghosts, or 'orbs,' on film at certain significant areas of the tour. The guide offers dramatic and historic accounts of locations such as the Ryman, State Capitol, and the Hermitage Hotel. The Haunted Downtown Tour has been featured on CBS, FOX, NBC, TLC, and in a variety of newspapers, magazines, and documentaries.

The Haunted Tavern Tour features the historic pubs and taverns in the entertainment district of 2nd Avenue and Broadway. The tour guide shares all of the haunted history and 'intoxicating' tales of the buildings visited. Designed to be a social tour, the guests enjoy drink discounts and a game of haunted trivia for prizes throughout the evening. This haunted pub-crawl has been a favorite for company outings and bachelor/bachelorette parties.

*For more information about Nashville Ghost Tours, call (615) 884-3999 or visit its web site at www.nashvilleghosttours.com.*

# I

# Old Hickory Rides Again

Even though Tennessee has been the home of three different Presidents, it's Andrew Jackson who has always been the most popular with Nashville residents. Office buildings, schools, towns, roads, libraries, and lakes all bear some form of his name, his wife's name, or even the name of his estate, the Hermitage. History has painted Jackson as a fiery, swashbuckling war hero and the kind of man with the rare ability to inspire others to follow him into deadly battle. While these characterizations are accurate, this is only one shade of a complex man. His beloved wife, Rachel, saw a gentler side, and his home is a testament to his taste for the pleasantries of life.

His home, the Hermitage, lies on the east side of downtown in an area of Nashville aptly named "Hermitage." The road leading up to the mansion, with its carefully spaced cedars on either side, hint at the grandeur of the home it approaches. The driveway is unique in its shape of a guitar (fitting, for a city nicknamed "Music City"). The home itself harkens back to an age of the Old South. The white home, with massive columns and seemingly endless meadows peppered with wildflowers suggest a penchant for elegance from a long gone genteel era.

After Jackson passed away, his heirs didn't seem to share the same love for the estate as he did. They divided up his expensive furniture, fine china, and belongings like thieves splitting their loot, not concerned with sentimentality but only with immediate financial worth. It was not long before the Hermitage itself began to suffer from neglect. A shell of its former glory, at one point the Hermitage was used as a home for elderly Confederate veterans. While Jackson, a soldier himself, may have been pleased to have

**Statue of Andrew Jackson. This was the first equestrian statue built in the United States.**

seen his home used to care for America's war veterans, he would have been heartbroken to see his home in its sorry state in the late 1800s. The ornate wallpaper was peeling like a serpent shedding skin. The gardens, once tranquil and full of life, were completely consumed by weeds. Broken windows, torn carpet, and mold-covered ceilings told the story of negligence to any that entered.

A group of concerned women came together to discuss the future of the Hermitage. It was clear that if this disregard for the home was to continue, eventually the once grand plantation would be no more. The women formed the Ladies Hermitage Association and received a charter from the state of Tennessee. Their mission was to save and restore the home. They were given ownership of the estate in July of 1893.

There was some concern among them that because the home was empty, it could be looted or vandalized even further. They decided that someone should stay there until a full-time caretaker could be procured. Two of the ladies in the group, Mary Baxter and Mary Dorris, volunteered to stay there.

They journeyed to the Hermitage with enough clothing and supplies to stay for days. Upon viewing the dilapidated home surrounded by the bloom and radiance of a summer's day, the ladies were able to see past the damaged home. Like a sculptor viewing rough wood, they saw the beauty that might be carved out with some determination and work.

They were greeted by a man called Uncle Alfred Jackson. He was a black man who had been Andrew Jackson's valet and was still living in a cabin on the property. As he often did, he eagerly told of his stories of Andrew Jackson. The man was clearly proud of his connection with the history of the place, but at his elderly age and almost completely blind, he was unable to do anything about the erosion that had occurred within the house. Uncle Alfred was pleased to learn of the restoration they had planned.

When the ladies began to unpack their things and started setting up a makeshift camp with pallets in the middle of the main hall, Alfred asked what they were doing. The ladies explained that they intended to spend the night there for at least a couple of days. Alfred's face clearly showed a look of concern, which the ladies mistook for simple trepidation for their safety.

"I wouldn't stay here. Not after dark. It's too…it's just too…" he stammered looking for the words, "Strange things happen here at night."

"Vandals," one of the two Mary's said.

"Well, yes, some… but OTHER things, too. There are wild carryings on here. Noises, and…" Uncle Alfred looked at the two women, who had skeptical looks on their faces. "I just wouldn't recommend staying, if you can help it. This house is…" he looked back and forth over each shoulder, like a man about to share the most sacred of secrets, "it has phantoms. I swear. I've seen them myself, at least back when my eyes were stronger."

"Ghosts!" one of the ladies blurted in surprise.

The other Mary tried to assure him, "We appreciate your concern, but we can manage just fine. We're not easily frightened by night creatures and such."

"I see," Uncle Alfred said smiling thinly. They would have to learn for themselves. "At least let me see if I can find an extra lantern."

He ambled off with the small strides of a man clearly feeling the aches and pains of old age. Once out of sight, the two Mary's exchanged looks that said '*Poor man. His seclusion out here has clearly made him a bit fearful and superstitious.*' Uncle Alfred's apprehension about the ladies' overnight stay was treated like how a parent might listen to a young child's fantasies with patience and interest, but ultimately disregarded as foolishness.

As the blazing July sun began to mercifully submerge into the tree line, casting a long web of shadows about the plantation grounds, Uncle Alfred asked if he could be of any further help. He looked toward the sunset as he asked this, and it was clear they didn't need him. He hoped they were right. He bid them a good night's rest and started across the field, now full of the flickering fireflies, with a gait that seemed a bit faster than the ladies had seen earlier that day.

The sun finally disappeared over the hills, leaving only a purple tint in the sky as a clue that it was once there. Although they had been confident in their abilities to make it through the night there, the oncoming darkness pulled their deeply imbedded fears and nightmares to the surface. They spent the night talking with each other cheerily about renovations and their families, but all the while were aware of the sprawling shadows around them.

The home was quiet, except for the constant brushing sound made by the warm breeze blowing through the trees outside. As bedtime approached, the ladies went through the house with their lanterns to lock up the doors and windows. Secure in their safety from would-be thieves (or worse), the two Marys changed into their nightclothes and stretched out on their blankets for the night.

Despite Uncle Alfred's superstitious talk earlier, they had been fine. This made them feel a little better that nothing had occurred in their time here. They talked to each other for a while laying on their backs and staring at the tall ceiling above. They drifted off to sleep and dreamt of other things.

One of the women, Mrs. Baxter, was dreaming of a horse galloping over the meadows around the plantation. The horse was barely visible in the distance as it dipped down into a valley out of sight. The horse disappeared from her vision, but she could hear the faint thunder of its hooves as it approached. Again the horse emerged as it ascended another hill. The horse was not slender and fast but enormous. The horse's color was mostly white, but it was also splattered with splotches of gray. The rider was difficult to see at first, but was clearly male.

As the horse charged forward, the scene started to seem less tranquil—it was becoming more threatening. The horse seemed to be coming straight toward her, and in her dream she felt the first twinges of panic. Clouds of dust and clumps of dirt trailed the stallion with each gallop. The steed's eyes seemed to have an unhealthy pink color to them and saliva spewed from his mouth. And the rider...

She was certainly in the midst of a full-fledged nightmare now, and was starting to toss in her bed with sweat glistening on her skin. Mrs. Morris was out of her bed, clutching Mrs. Baxter's arms trying to wake her unsuccessfully.

In her dream, the horseman was dressed in the clothes of a military man, but the uniform seemed tattered and dingy. The sound of the horse's gallop was thunderous now, and again the horse disappeared behind another hill. It emerged much quicker this time and seemed impossibly close. The rider reached to his side and withdrew a sword. Unlike his worn uniform, his sword was pristine. She could almost hear the metal blade ring as it slid from its sheath. He held the silver saber over his head in a threatening and confident posture.

She could see his eyes. They were sunken in, but looking right at her. His face was gray and flaked, like damaged leather. She realized with horror that the man was dead.

He called out, "Mary!" And in her dream state, she knew that he was there to kill her. "Mary!" he barked again and she closed her eyes, braced for the impact of his sword.

"Mary, wake up! Someone is here!"

Mary Baxter stirred awake, confused as her eyes adjusted to the sight of her friend hovering above her with a look of concern and fear.

"What? Wait, wait, I'm awake," but this was barely true. She was starting to feel the first relief one gets when it's realized that a nightmare is just a nightmare. That relief didn't last long.

From the kitchen came the unmistakable sound of a pile of dishes crashing to the floor. A moment later another crash, possibly a tea set, made the startled ladies grab at each other. They huddled together in one another's grip like children with their eyes wide trying to see through the darkness. The noise of what sounded like silverware being tossed across the room made them only tighten their grip on each other.

The woman, who had been suffering the nightmare, looked at her friend, Mary Morris and said, "A thief in the kitchen?"

"I don't think so," Mrs. Morris whispered. As if in confirmation of her answer, she became aware of another sound from just outside on the porch. It sounded as if heavy chains were dragging across the wooden floors, making long scratching and clanging noises as they passed. From their pallet in the parlor, they looked toward the windows in the direction of the porch, thinking maybe the moon would reveal the image of someone there, but it didn't.

"Oh, no. It's coming back, Mary," and before Mary Baxter could ask exactly *what* was coming back, she heard it herself. Her stomach seemed to sink through the floor as she heard the first sound of hooves on the floor above them. Shortly removed from her dream, the emotions of helplessness and doom came flooding quickly back to the surface.

The horse whined loudly, and they could imagine the horse reared back on his hind legs. Deafening clapping sounds traced across the floor above them. The unseen horse must have barged into walls and rails all along the way, considering the commotion it caused as it crossed the long hallway of the home. The sound stopped and then continued again in the other direction. One of the Mary's fumbled for the lantern, and tried to light it. This proved difficult because each bang or crash only made her fingers tremble more.

Finally, the lantern was lit, revealing the parlor to them in its glow. The sounds were gone. The orange glow of the lantern revealed their pale faces and watery eyes.

Neither of them could bring themselves to investigate the upstairs, kitchen, or porch that night. They started to speculate as to what happened, but neither acknowledged the possibility of a ghost out loud. Maybe the thief or thieves had run away once they realized someone was there. Maybe it had been rats scurrying upstairs or wild dogs that had somehow made their way inside.

They comforted each other with a variety of theories throughout the night. They felt confident that there was a rational explanation for the event, although without word neither turned out the kerosene lantern for the rest of the night.

The next morning, with the security of the sunlight, they walked through the house. They first checked the kitchen, because it seemed most likely to have suffered the most damage, fully expecting to find a floor immersed in a variety of twinkling shards of glass and broken pieces of irreplaceable china. They were both relieved – and confused – to find the kitchen to be in the same condition as before. They looked at each other in disbelief and then scanned the kitchen again with their eyes to confirm their first evaluation.

After opening a couple of cabinets to be sure, they silently went upstairs. Again, the second floor, although damaged from decades of abuse and filth, was no different than the day before.

They settled on a theory that combined the idea of rats, their heightened fear due to Uncle Alfred's ghost stories, and the accentuated acoustics of the empty home. In the daytime, this sounded perfectly reasonable, although internally they each harbored their doubts.

They spent the rest of the day not talking of ghosts and phantom horses, but doing some preliminary cleaning and assessing the work to be done. After lunch they took a break to read in the garden near Andrew and Rachel Jackson's tomb. While reading their books, they would occasionally glance toward their graves, wondering about the night before.

That evening they settled down again for bed as before, except this time they left the lantern on. Regardless, later that evening the sounds came back again with force, waking the women from their sleep. They listened as the chains rattled and the creature upstairs crossed back and forth for a few minutes. Eventually, it stopped.

This happened night after night, making it impossible to get a good night's sleep. They saw Uncle Alfred intermittently throughout their time there, but never told him of their late night visitations. They finally hired a full time custodian to care for the plantation and were able to return home. They couldn't have been happier.

Weeks later the ladies were at the house cleaning the walls. They had not told their families or anyone about their experiences and had managed to think of those nights there less and less. They were working in one of the bedrooms and had pulled back some furniture from the wall. There had been ample evidence of drifters and squatters throughout the house, and as indicated by the graffiti now revealed on the wall, they weren't the only ones to have heard the nighttime sounds. In large capital letters, someone had written a single word. It was amazing how the single name etched there told them all they needed to know about this long gone wanderer's stay here.

**ICHABOD**

The ladies looked at each other shaking their heads. Both were well read women, and they each knew the story of Ichabod Crane and his ghostly headless horseman. Apparently, someone else had a similar experience and felt the need to pass along this message – or warning – to other would-be visitors.

As time passed, days turning into weeks and weeks into years, they shared their stories with others—and they each had come to the conclusion that there must have been a ghost. The most likely identity was that of Andrew Jackson himself. They thought it was Jackson that had been riding throughout his home on his horse. Was he protecting the home? Could it be that his spirit was restless and angered by the way his cherished retreat had decayed over time? It seemed so to the two Mary's.

They never slept in the home again and were unsure if the restorations they made had pleased him, allowing his spirit to rest or not. No matter how fantastic or remarkable events in life can be, things always have a way of getting back to normal, and this was the case for these two women. Their lives rolled on. The ladies returned to their worlds of child-rearing and husbands. They continued to attend church and visit friends. They worked, ran their homes, watched friends marry, watched friends die, cooked, lived, laughed, and cried. The seemingly supernatural encounters with Jackson's ghost were not life altering. Their religions and outlook on life stayed very much the same.

For Mary Baxter, the experience had become little more than an anecdote in her past. It was a ghost story that became a favorite of her children's. At night before bed and after prayers, the children would often beg their mother to again tell them the story of the ghost horse. Most nights, Mary would decline, not wanting to ruin their sleep.

On rare nights, when her defenses were down, she would sometimes tell them her story of the haunted home, her dream, and the galloping horse with its enigmatic rider. This would please the children, who always gladly went to sleep afterwards. Mary would cover the young ones, pulling the blankets carefully up to their chins. She would look back at them from the doorway with immeasurable love, careful to leave their lantern lit as she left. Just in case.

# 2

# The State Capitol

## Fighting Spirits

Perched on the tallest hill in downtown Nashville rests the Tennessee State Capitol building. Overlooking the War Memorial Plaza, the structure looks more like a Greek temple than a state office building. During daylight hours the grounds are abuzz with legislators, reporters, and often school groups from all over Tennessee visiting their State Capitol building. At night however, the mood and feel of the area is vastly different. The mammoth ionic columns and grand marble stairs, which seem so splendid during the day, look far more ominous and cold against the backdrop of the night sky. Especially eerie are the grounds around the building. There are trees, statues of Tennessee heroes, and monuments all over the property, connected by a network of paths and steep stairways. As the sun sets, long shadows are cast, playing tricks on the mind. Adding to the mood of the area are hundreds of small bats that come zigzagging about to feed on the insects.

Bats are not the only creatures said to roam this hill. There has been talk among locals for decades that ghosts are lurking in the hallways and grounds of the Tennessee State Capitol.

In fact, the building has been haunted almost since it was first constructed, because one of the ghosts at the sight is the architect who designed it. William Strickland, a world famous architect from Pennsylvania, restored Independence Hall in Philadelphia and was an apprentice to the architect who designed the U.S. Capitol building. He was considered to be one of the top architects in the world when he was hired to design Tennessee's Capitol.

**The Tennessee State Capitol Building is the site of many of the city's most well known ghosts.**

Strickland was the type of architect who was always trying to be a master of the latest trends, and at that time Greek revival was very popular. This is the reason he designed the building to resemble a Greek temple. They broke ground in 1845 and Strickland believed he would be home in just a few years. He was wrong. There were several delays and problems with the construction project. Strickland died April 7, 1854, but the building was not completed until 1859. His son, Francis Strickland, helped finish the construction after his father passed away.

One of the reasons the construction lasted so long was because of a local politician named Samuel Morgan. Morgan was in charge of the budget on the project, and it's said that he and Strickland could not agree on how to complete it. Of course Samuel Morgan was more interested in bringing everything in under budget, and in Strickland's opinion, sacrificing quality in materials. Strickland believed this building to be his lifetime masterpiece and wanted it to last for generations. The two men were known to get into heated arguments, right in front of the laborers on the state property. Both men were stubborn and would get into stalemates refusing to budge. These disagreements would bring construction to a screeching halt, sometimes for months. By the time William Strickland died in 1854, he and Morgan were enemies not only in business, but also on a personal level.

Because William Strickland had essentially given his life to Nashville, the city bestowed a great and rare honor to him. They allowed him to be entombed within the State Capitol building itself. He even designed his own vault, always intending to be buried there...just not so soon. His remains are in the cornerstone of the structure, and that's where he will remain as long as the Capitol stands. However, this rare honor given to Strickland was not completely an exclusive one. There is one other individual who is buried in the Capitol. That man is Samuel Morgan. It's this situation — two enemies being buried here together — that has caused all of the ghost stories to emerge in the years afterward.

**The tomb of William Strickland, architect of the State Capitol.**

The belief is that these two men are so distressed at being buried here together that they are still fighting and arguing with each other in the afterlife as ghosts.

Many of the eyewitnesses over the years have been Metro police officers. It's a common early assignment for rookie police officers to work as security guards at the Capitol. Most of those police officers interviewed have come away believing that some of the spirits are not at rest there.

One particular Nashville police officer shared his story. On one evening, he was patrolling the grounds when out of the darkness he heard a heated argument between two men. As protocol dictated, he radioed in for backup. Other policemen arrived promptly. They fanned out and did a sweep of the area, but were unable to find anyone. The officer assumed the men must have slipped away in the shadows somehow. This was the first, but hardly the last time, that this officer had this type of encounter. Over the following months, he reported hearing these arguments again and again. Each time he would call for backup, but somehow these two men were eluding capture. The young officer was baffled by what was happening, but began to see a pattern. The arguments always seemed to occur close to 9 p.m. He was sharing this story with an older veteran officer, who began to smile and nod knowingly. The rookie mistook the smile as patronizing and was insulted.

"What's so funny about that?" he asked, thinking the veteran officer was making fun of his inability to apprehend these trespassers.

"I'm not laughing at you. In fact I had the same thing happen when I was a rookie up there. But you'll never capture those two."

Puzzled the rookie asked, "Why not?"

The older officer smiled even wider and raised an eyebrow, "Because those aren't *men* fighting up there. You're looking for ghosts."

There are several other policemen, who have been interviewed, that have had similar experiences. Many of them claim that the arguing between Strickland and Morgan is so common that it becomes almost ordinary and expected...

like part of the background. Most don't even call in the disturbances anymore.

Although most accounts of these two spirits involve only hearing them argue, there are stories of a more physical nature. One police officer related a story in which he was driving up the road that winds around and circles the back of the Capitol late in the afternoon. As he was approaching the corner where William Strickland's tomb rested on his left, to the right he saw a large stone fly out of the tree line. His jaw dropped at the sight of this rock sailing through the air. The trajectory of the stone would have it on course to crash into the wall where Strickland's tomb rested. As it hurtled across the blue sky in front of his squad car, the policeman watched on helplessly. Amazingly it stopped, and according to him, it hung in the air for just a moment before crashing to the ground below. The officer believed that what he witnessed on that day was another one of their feuds, and that Morgan had thrown the rock at Strickland's tomb, but that Strickland had grabbed the stone defending his resting place.

Strange things have occurred inside the building as well. Security tells stories of computer printers turning on by themselves and printing out blank sheets of paper, echoes of unexplained footsteps, and moving shadows. A common occurrence is for security to be patrolling through a particular room on the top floor; as they enter, the door will close and lock behind them, leaving them trapped. They ultimately have to radio for help to get out, which doesn't cause any real harm other than to their pride.

# forever on Guard

Not all are aware that Nashville and the surrounding areas have a very rich Civil War history. There were several key battles including the Battle of Franklin and the Battle of Nashville. At one point in 1862, the Union army seized the Tennessee State Capitol building and fortified it. It was called Fort Andrew Johnson. This site was a strategically sound location for two main reasons. One is that on the hill, they could see for miles in any direction, able to see if enemy troops were approaching. The other is that the cannons and bunkers that surrounded the building served not only as protection, but also intimidated the citizens below, and at least subconsciously those citizens were aware that the cannons could devastate the city should a revolt have occurred.

Shortly after the building was seized by the Union, a small band of Rebels made an effort to try and reclaim it but failed. There was a fierce conflict and several men lost their lives beneath the trees surrounding the Capitol. There are still some bullet holes in the doors of the Capitol because of that skirmish.

It's believed one of the Union officers who died that day is still patrolling the grounds in the afterlife as a ghost. This soldier can appear day or night and has been encountered inside and outside of the Capitol building. His temperament is different compared to the ghosts in most stories. In many ways, ghosts are often benign. They are seen crossing rooms or sliding objects across tables, but rarely involve themselves directly with the living. This ghostly soldier is far more aggressive.

One such account involved a painter who was redecorating an office. At lunch time the rest of the crew decided to go out to eat. Exhausted, the painter chose to stay behind and take a quick nap instead. The man settled onto a small couch in the office, propped his feet up on a coffee table, and drifted off to sleep with his cap pulled halfway down his face. A short time later he was awakened after feeling two hands clutching him around the ankles. His legs were thrown off the table with rude force. The painter's eyes popped open, and to his dismay a bearded man was leering over him, dressed in a blue Union officer's uniform.

"Keep your feet off the furniture!" the soldier barked at the painter. The painter jumped from the couch, his cap falling to the ground. He shook his head and quickly rubbed his eyes. In less than a second, the soldier was gone. Was he dreaming? Had the soldier slipped away? He didn't think so.

Others have had similar experiences with this officer. Always described as angry and forceful, the soldier will appear to the unsuspecting, barking orders at them. He's also physically imposing and he's been known to shove people, grab them by the shoulders, or throw them to the ground.

There are patterns to what triggers his appearances. He seems to show himself when someone is in the act of rearranging furniture, accidentally knocking an object off a table, or in many cases vandalizing the property. One security guard recalled an evening in which he witnessed on a security camera three young men vandalizing one of the walls on the grounds. He rushed down to the site to find the three of them terrified. One of the teenagers was sitting in the grass clearly dazed rubbing the back of his head.

One of the boys spotted the security guard, "Hey, we're going to sue you and your partner."

The officer had no idea what the vandal was talking about. He didn't have a partner. Later the three youths told the officer their story. They claimed that moments before he arrived, another policeman dressed in blue had come "out of nowhere" and had started yelling and shoving them around. One of the boys stumbled backward falling into the base of a tree, smacking the back of his head. As quickly as he appeared, the man was gone. Unaware of the Capitol ghost stories, the boys believed it had been an actual policeman that had roughed them up. The security guard knew better. He suspected that the boys had mistaken the blue Union uniform for a policeman's attire.

It appears that any event that changes the status quo at the Capitol building stirs this soldier and draws him forward. It's as if he is still trying to defend the hill...much as he had in that battle.

## Polk's Tomb

President James K. Polk and his wife Sarah lived at Sarah's home, known as Polk Place, on 8th Avenue, just a few blocks from the state Capitol building. Polk died in June 1849 from a bout with cholera. Sarah passed away many years later in 1891. Both were entombed on their property. In the year of Sarah Polk's death, the Polk Place was sold to Jacob McGavock Dickinson. Heated debate followed among Nashvillians about what should happen to the tomb of James and Sarah Polk, which was designed by William Strickland, the same man who had designed the Capitol.

The tomb of President James K. Polk and his wife Sarah located on the State Capitol grounds.

Ultimately it was decided to move the entire tomb structure to the state property grounds near the statue of Andrew Jackson. They even chose to unearth both bodies and rebury them within the tomb.

There are two things that make President James K. Polk noteworthy. One is that he is still the only U.S. President to write down all of his campaign promises, and once he was elected fulfilled each and every promise that he made. The other involves his wife Sarah. Often when they had to attend a banquet or gala, President Polk would make his entrance unnoticed. He was a shorter man at 5'6" and would occasionally not be seen upon entering the room. The result was that often the guests would not stand showing respect at his arrival.

This was irritating to Sarah, so one evening at a special event she approached the band leader early telling him, "I want you to play 'Hail to the Chief' when the President makes his entrance tonight." When Polk entered that night, they played the song. Everyone stood immediately, realizing that the President was there. It's said that this is where the tradition of playing 'Hail to the Chief' at a President's entrance originated.

The ghost story of the tomb is that over the years, people have claimed to see a man in a dark suit kneeling at the base of the crypt. As the curious witnesses approach the grave, the image of the man seems to evaporate and disappear. Of course, no one can be certain who this mysterious man is, but most suspect that it's President Polk himself. It does make some sense that he may not be happy with having his resting place tampered with in such a manner.

## Rachel in the Tower

One of Nashville's most beloved female figures is Rachel Jackson. Born Rachel Donelson, she married future President, Andrew Jackson. Their love affair was famous. Their marriage was not simply one of political convenience, but by all accounts was a passionate and fiery relationship. Both Andrew and Rachel spent a great deal of time in the city. Rachel herself

**Rachel Jackson, tragic figure and adored wife of President Andrew Jackson.**

Rachel Jackson's ghost is said to haunt the State Capitol's tower.

was a socialite, and spent a great deal of time visiting friends in the downtown area. Andrew Jackson's law office was located in the heart of the city, just a few streets from the Capitol building.

When Andrew declared his candidacy for the presidential election, the newspapers reported that Rachel had been married before she had married Andrew. This made her marriage to Jackson illegal, which scandalized her with polite society. She lost all of her friends, and social circles ostracized her completely. Andrew was one of the few that stuck by her.

The last few months of her life were sad and lonely. She died of heart failure the night before Andrew left town to be inaugurated in Washington D.C. on December 22, 1828. So Rachel was never able to see her husband become President or become First Lady herself. She was buried in her garden at their home, the Hermitage. When Andrew died years later, he was buried alongside her in a Greek inspired tomb.

Anywhere you find tragedy like this you often find ghost stories as well. Rachel is not only said to haunt her home, the Hermitage, at night by playing the piano there, but witnesses claim she also haunts the State Capitol tower. There are hundreds of eyewitness accounts of this over the years, due to the fact that the tower is so visible from all around the city. As business people are walking to their offices or sitting in traffic, they will glance toward the tower and see a solitary woman there. She's most often described as wearing a maroon or brown dress with her hair pulled back. After a moment the woman turns and walks out of sight, leaving the witnesses to wonder if they have seen the ghost of Rachel Jackson.

# 3

# The Hermitage Hotel

T he Hermitage Hotel is the only five-diamond hotel in the downtown area. Its historic qualities and preserved beauty make it a significant landmark in Nashville. Named after President Andrew Jackson's home, the Hermitage, the hotel opened September 17, 1910. For the first half of that century, this hotel was the hot spot of downtown Nashville. Anyone of political power or celebrity status would typically stay at the Hermitage Hotel.

This site has hosted a variety of famous guests including Greta Garbo, Bette Davis, Gene Autry, Sgt. Alvin York, and Al Capone. It has also seen six U.S. Presidents: Taft, Roosevelt, Wilson, Johnson, Nixon, and Kennedy. Minnesota Fats, the famous pool hustler, lived at this hotel in the 1940s and then again in the 1980s when he died. It's said he made quite a living hustling tourists on a pool table located in the mezzanine. Dinah Shore began her musical career on a radio program that was broadcast out of what is now the hotel's Capitol Grille in 1946. Besides celebrities, it has also been an important site for political reasons. Because of its proximity to the Capitol building, there have often been political conventions, key speeches, and rallies held there. It was also the headquarters for both sides of the Women's Suffrage movement in Tennessee.

The structure itself is a work of art. Although the hotel was renovated and restored in 2000, much of the character and original décor has been saved. The lobby is breathtaking with the cut, stained glass on the ceiling and the magnificent flooring made of Italian sienna marble. Russian walnut wood panels the walls. It was originally decorated with enormous, stuffed furniture and

**The Hermitage Hotel is one of the most historic sites in downtown Nashville.**

Notorious pool shark Minnesota Fats once had a pool table in the mezzanine provided by the Hermitage Hotel where he often hustled tourists out of money.

Persian rugs. The hotel itself is a step into a more elegant past. Perhaps this is why so many spirits seem to feel so comfortable staying here.

# Room 910

One of the ghosts can be found on the very top floor in room 910. These accounts date back to the early 1960s. One such encounter involved a man that used to be a bellhop there. He was carrying up luggage for some guests that had just arrived at the hotel. With bags under each arm, he lumbered towards 910 and began to hear the cry of a baby. The bellhop set the heavy luggage down on the floor and knocked on the door. No one was supposed to be inside. He waited. No one came. He knocked again and again... the child's cries grew more intense with each passing moment.

The bellhop began to suspect that the child was in some sort of danger. He fished out a large ring of keys from his pocket. He slid the key into the lock and began to turn the knob. In the split second that he cracked the door open, the crying stopped. He rushed into the room and searched under the bed, closets, and bathroom. The room was vacant. Terrified, the bellhop ran from the room. Bypassing the elevator, he ran down all nine flights of stairs to the lobby. The bellhop threw his keys at the front desk clerk and continued out the front door. Days later, he refused to return to work, despite the urging of his employers.

Today, hotel guests on the top floor will often call down to the front desk to complain of a crying sound next door saying, "I think there's something wrong next door. There's a child that's been crying all night, like she's been left alone." The hotel guests' concern is genuine because they are often unaware of the building's haunted history. The front desk clerks, however, are familiar with the ghost stories, but **NEVER** mention them. "Thank you for calling. We will send someone right away." This is, of course, a lie. The clerks know there is no point in sending anyone to the room, because they are able to look at the registry and see that the room is unoccupied...at least by the living.

It's interesting to note that room 910 no longer exists. If one were to visit the hotel today or request that room number, those efforts would be futile. Just before 2000, the hotel was purchased. In years prior, there had been mismanagement and the hotel had been in disrepair. It had lost its luster and was on the verge of being condemned. The investors had to pour in millions of dollars to renovate and restore the Hermitage Hotel to its former grandeur. Several upgrades were made to modernize the hotel and to make it profitable. One decision was to have a grand presidential suite on the top floor. The wall between rooms 910 and 912 was torn down combining the two into what is now one of the largest and most expensive rooms in the building. It usually costs over $2,000 a night.

## The Lady in White

Whereas the spirit of 910 haunts only that room when it's vacant, not all of the hotel's ghosts are as particular about which areas of the hotel they can be found. The Lady in White is one of the hotel's more free-roaming specters. She has been witnessed on every floor, and in the guest rooms, hallways, and lobby. The Lady in White's name has been lost to us, which is why she's known by the nickname, and because she's always described as wearing a white dress. She's said to have been wearing this white dress when she was found dead.

Although her name is unknown to historians, her story isn't. It has been passed down from one generation to the next and continues to grow with each passing decade. What is known is that she died in 1911, just a year after the Hermitage Hotel opened its doors. The story is that the Lady in White was staying at the hotel with her husband, a man believed to have been a state politician. She left the hotel to go sight-seeing all afternoon, but she came back several hours earlier than he expected her to.

She entered the hotel room and was shocked to discover her husband in the arms of another woman. Due to their loud arguments over the next few days, the other guests at the hotel became aware of the situation. Gossip and speculation about the tawdry affair spread through the hotel.

A few days later, the fighting stopped.

A maid entered the room to find a lady dressed in white hanged to death. The cleaning woman's screams could be heard throughout the hotel. Soon, police were everywhere, but there was not a suicide note to be found. This led to the possibility that perhaps her husband had killed her, staging it to appear as if she had killed herself in her grief. After a few weeks of investigating, her murder was deemed a suicide. Some have speculated that this was a cover up due to his political position.

Most employees at the Hermitage Hotel have come to believe that he had killed her because her spirit is still not at rest and continues to haunt the hotel almost a century later. Her image is always described to appear transparent. She never speaks. If someone calls out to her, it's like she's unaware that anyone is there. The Lady in White is also very graceful and mobile. Accounts of her appearances almost seem as if she's floating and gliding from place to place.

A front desk clerk recalled a strange encounter in the summer of 2005. A lady checked into the hotel alone and was given room 813. Late that evening, this woman awakened to the sound of a door opening and closing. She sat up in her bed with a quickened pulse. No one was there. She was staying by herself, and reasoned that she must have heard the echo from another door down the hall. She settled back into bed, secure in her safety, and fell back into a light sleep.

A few moments later, she was awakened again by feeling someone sitting down on the foot of her bed. Holding her breath, she carefully peered over the covers. To her amazement, the woman could see the back of another lady sitting on the edge of her own bed. Frozen in horror, she watched as this uninvited lady stood and crossed the room. She followed the intruder with her eyes as she approached the door. Unbelievably, the woman did not open the door — but walked straight *THROUGH* the wall, as if it weren't even there.

The front desk clerk answered the phone downstairs. Between cries and hysterics, the woman in 813 relayed the experience to the clerk. The clerk had only been working at the hotel for a few weeks at that point and was unaware of the building's haunted history. She assumed that the woman was either a little crazy, or had perhaps had one too many martinis. She wrote the whole experience off as the imagination of an eccentric hotel guest...until the following week when she had the exact same complaint from a different man. He also was staying in room 813 and had no prior knowledge of the ghost story. Their experiences were nearly identical, especially the detail about a woman sitting at the foot of the bed.

Why is this woman still wandering the halls of the hotel? Is she searching for something? Maybe she seeks revenge or answers to her death.

## The Southern Belle

The head of security for the Hermitage Hotel scanned the crowd with mild interest. All in attendance at the cocktail party wore black ties and elegant evening gowns. The lobby

The lobby of the Hermitage Hotel is often the site of black tie affairs that are visited by the mysterious Southern Belle spirit.

**Most often the Southern Belle ghost is seen in the balconies above the lobby watching guests below.**

of the hotel always had a regal feel to it, but especially so that night. Flowers and music filled the room as the guests mingled, laughing and chatting with champagne glasses in hand. How much money had this event cost? Forty thousand? Fifty? Maybe more.

The guard shifted from one foot to the other wondering how long this party would last. Suddenly, he felt a cold draft come over him. Had the air conditioning just turned on? He looked around unable to find an air vent anywhere nearby. "How could it have gotten so cold?" he wondered. The curious drop in temperature quickly left the guard's mind as he looked across the crowded lobby.

There stood what he later believed to be the most beautiful woman that he had ever seen in his life. This dark-haired beauty walked down a short flight of stairs and began to cross the room in his direction. As she made her way across the floor, he realized that he was not the only one to notice this woman's good looks. Men would stop in mid-sentence, mouth's agape in an almost comical pose, as they would watch this mysterious woman pass by in her green, southern belle gown. One lady actually lightly punched the shoulder of her escort to snap him out of his daze.

The woman in green seemed unaware of the eyes of everyone around her. Perhaps she was accustomed to this sort of attention, or maybe there was another reason for her seeming oblivious. As she made her way through the crowd, the guard noticed her captivating watery blue eyes and her white skin that made him think of Carolina sands.

It appeared that she was approaching him specifically. His pulse quickened as he realized this stunning woman was looking at *him*. What could she want with him? He looked over his shoulder, half expecting to see her handsome, Rhett Butleresque date to be standing there waiting for her. The stairs behind him were empty. He turned back to the party, but the woman was gone.

He looked from right to left, but he couldn't locate this lady who had simply disappeared. The guard felt a little sting in his heart, like puppy love lost. How silly, he realized, it was to feel loss over this stranger that he didn't even know.

Regardless, he spent the rest of the evening looking for her, but he didn't see her again that night or in the years afterward, although he said he always hoped he would.

Sightings like this one have been reported almost since the hotel was first constructed. The Southern Belle is always encountered on the bottom two floors of the building. She's been seen in the restaurant, in the lobby, and most often on the veranda overlooking the lobby below. It's also more common for her to emerge when there are large groups present. It's almost as if she's a bit of a socialite and has frequently been viewed leaning against the railing, watching guests in the lobby below.

The identity of this woman is debated among those affiliated with the hotel, with four or five possible theories. Whoever she was, it seems that she probably passed on before the hotel was constructed. By all accounts her style of dress would place her more in the 1800s rather than after 1910 when the hotel opened.

Perhaps she lived and died in one of the older homes there back when the area was mostly residential. She could have haunted that home until it was torn down and the area was developed for more metropolitan types of sites, like the Hermitage Hotel. This would at least explain why she only haunts the bottom two floors of the building, because her home wouldn't have been any taller than that.

Whatever the case, the Southern Belle continues to enchant those who see her to this day.

# 4

# The Lost Tomb of St. Mary of the Seven Sorrows

St. Mary of the Seven Sorrows is the oldest church in downtown Nashville. It was the first Catholic church in middle Tennessee. Nestled between more modern skyscrapers and characterless office buildings, this church has often been overlooked by locals. The church itself was an architectural triumph when built by William Strickland, architect of the State Capitol building. This church, influenced by Greek revival, was considered a marvel for its absence of support beams or columns in the interior of the church. Ironically, the church was dedicated on Halloween of 1847.

Over the years, priests at the church had numerous encounters that led them to believe that something strange was happening within their walls. For decades they kept their dark stories secret, only sharing them with each other. These supernatural tales finally came to public light in published magazine articles in 1973.

This ghost story really begins with a lady named Nell Hines. She had been a cook at the church for many years during the Great Depression. One evening after dinner, while she was cleaning and putting away dishes in the kitchen area, Nell glanced up to see a priest enter the room.

He was unfamiliar to her, so she called out, "Hello?" The priest did not respond. The man began to cross the room towards an opposite door unresponsive to Nell's call.

"Sir? Are you lost? Can I help you?" Nell asked louder. Either the man was deaf or intentionally ignoring her. She placed the dishes she was holding on a nearby table, wiped her hands on her apron, and started towards him.

St. Mary of the Seven Sorrows is the oldest church in Nashville and served as a Civil War hospital for both Union and Confederate soldiers. Three hundred young men died at this location.

**For decades the bells in the tower have been ringing all hours of the night, leaving many priests to conclude that the building is haunted.**

His most striking feature was his height. He was well over six feet tall, and she thought he might have to duck his head to exit the room. He walked with a cane and wore a hat, which barely cleared the doorframe as he left.

Nell hurried after him through the passage. He was gone. She was stunned. How could this man have disappeared? Nell left the room to approach the other priests about what she believed to be an intruder. She told her story to Father Duffy. As Nell described her experience, his heart began to race. He also thought that this man might have been some sort of thief or imposter. He ordered everyone to search the church for this trespasser. They were unable to find the man

Nell had described. Everything seemed to be in order, and nothing was stolen.

He theorized to Nell that perhaps she simply hadn't recognized one of their own priests in the shadows. Nell protested, claiming that she had a good look at him.

Over the years, Nell would see this man around the church. Each time she tried to speak to or catch the man, she would fail. He was so elusive and always seemed to duck around a corner or down a flight of stairs before she arrived. She always shared her stories and became almost obsessed with this mystery man. Initially people took her seriously, but over time everyone came to dismiss her as being overly imaginative. Although they internally scoffed and rolled their eyes at her stories, they would always appear to listen patiently, but they were only feigning interest and concern.

Eventually others besides Nell would see this man who was haunting St. Mary's. John Walker was a custodian at the church and on countless late nights he could be found sweeping the floors of the church. On repeated nights, he would be mopping the floors or dusting the pews when in the corner of his eye he would see movement. There in the center aisle was a priest, enormous in height, carrying a ceremonial staff towards the main altar. Alone and with only the aid of candlelight, John would rub his eyes and look again. The priest would disappear down the aisle, and he began to wonder if he too was losing his mind like many joked that Nell had.

It wasn't long before the priests in the church began to witness this man. Father Duffy claimed to have had numerous encounters he could not explain. One evening he was in the study reading a book when he heard a long, grinding creak. It was the screech of a door hinge in need of oil. He peered over his reading glasses and watched the heavy door slowly open. There was nothing there but darkness.

"The wind," Duffy said softly and returned to his book.

There was a soft shuffling sound, and then another, and another. Father Duffy looked up again, but no one was there—at least no one that he could see with his eyes. The sound of footsteps crossed the floor, and in the light radiance of the crackling fireplace, he thought he could almost see someone in the shadows. A door on the opposite end of the room opened and closed with a soft clicking sound of a door latch. It was as if an invisible man had casually crossed the room.

Father Duffy was unable to move and silently offered up a prayer.

Another priest, Father Cashin, claimed that over the years there were many strange happenings within St. Mary's. He alleged that he constantly heard knocking sounds and footsteps, but the most common occurrence was the ringing of the bells in the church tower. Late at night, the deep tolls of the bells would start ringing loudly, waking everyone from their sleep. The priests in the rectory would jump out of bed and rush up the long spiral staircase to the bell tower. Once they reached the top, the tower was always empty. Father Cashin believed this was impossible. He said there was no chance that anyone could make it from the bell tower to the base of the stairs before one of the other priests arrived. Cashin said that this was impossible for another reason. The bells had been broken for years and shouldn't have been capable of ringing at all.

Despite all of these incredible experiences, the most frightening occurred to Monsignor Morgan. He was asleep in his quarters in the rectory one night when he was awakened by a loud knocking at his door. Morgan sat up in bed reaching for a robe. His heart sank. Late night visits almost always meant that the messenger was bringing bad news. In a sense, he was right.

Morgan stumbled toward the door, unable to imagine what kind of dire report awaited him. He opened the door, but no one was there. The heavy doors at both ends of the hall were closed. Morgan knew that if those doors had opened, he would have heard them, but he hadn't. The knock at his door had not been his imagination, and the rumors of the church's ghost stories quickly sprung to mind. Frightened, Morgan slunk down into a large chair and pulled out a cigarette with trembling fingers. He lit it and stared anxiously at the door, wondering if someone was going to come back.

He sat there for nearly an hour too rattled to sleep. Eventually, he calmed himself down enough to go back to bed. He pulled the covers over himself and settled in, believing that the experience was over. He was wrong.

Again, Morgan was awakened by another heavy knocking sound, but this time it was not at his door but at the headboard just inches above his head. Morgan screamed and was halfway across the room in a flash, eyes blinking rapidly in the dark trying to see who was there. The room, like the hallway before, was empty except for Monsignor Morgan. He didn't sleep for the rest of the night.

He shared his story the next morning with all of the other priests. Tragically, Morgan died three days later from a heart attack while visiting the Nashville City Cemetery. This led to speculation that perhaps there was a connection between Monsignor Morgan's death and his encounter with St. Mary's ghost. One idea was that maybe the frightening encounter had placed too much stress on his heart. There was also the well-known superstition that a ghost knocking at your door was a sign of one's impending doom.

Clergy and caretakers at St. Mary's would share their stories with each other, but would rarely talk about their experiences outside of the church. One of the reasons for their secrecy was that they weren't certain who was causing the disturbances. There had been numerous deaths within the church. In the early years, one priest had fallen from a window to his death, another died from complications involving a Civil War injury years earlier, and a few others had died of natural causes.

Also, both Union and Confederate soldiers had used the building as a hospital throughout the Civil War. Over three hundred young men died on St. Mary's floors. Lying on their backs in the main part of the church, many of the soldier's last views were of the nine ceiling paintings, which include Matthew, Mark, Luke, John, The Last Supper, The Birth of Christ, Jesus taken down from the Cross, Jesus Praying in the Garden of Gethsemane, and Jesus in the Temple. It was the hope of some within the church that those paintings may have provided some comfort in the soldiers' time of pain.

Because there had been so much death within the church, no one could be certain who the ghost was or what was causing these strange happenings. Most of them believed that the ghost was one of the priests from the early years of the church... because he seemed to *still* be carrying out his priestly duties in the afterlife.

The identity of this spirit would have remained a mystery forever—except for an amazing discovery in 1969. St. Mary of the Seven Sorrows was in poor condition at this time and needed a complete overhaul to spare it from being condemned by the city. Electricians were tearing through the floor behind the main altar when they stumbled upon an astonishing site. It was the tomb of Bishop Richard Pius Miles. He had been the first bishop of Nashville and was present when the church had opened in 1847. Miles had died in 1860, but there had not been any record as to what had become of Bishop Miles' remains.

Unsure of what to do, the electricians notified the church of their discovery. The priests were stunned to learn of this tomb, and many rushed to the site to see for themselves. The tomb structure itself was very large. On the top was a sliding panel that, once opened, allowed one to see the face of the corpse inside. Many of the area's priests of the day viewed the remains of Bishop Miles and were shocked by his appearance. They claimed that Miles looked alive— that he hadn't decayed in the slightest. This was of course astonishing because Bishop Miles had been **DEAD** for over a hundred years at this point. Other than a greenish tint to his skin, they said it appeared that he might open his eyes any second.

In Catholic tradition, lack of decomposition is one of the signs of sainthood. It's one of the many indicators that a priest may be worthy of that title. This has led many of St. Mary's modern church members to believe that he's not only the ghost that haunted the building, but also that, one day, he may be recognized as a saint. Whoever buried the bishop must have thought him worthy of sainthood as well. That is why his tomb had been equipped with the sliding view window, so that future generations could check the decomposition levels of Miles to determine if he should be canonized.

**Bishop Richard Pius Miles may be the source for St. Mary's ghostly experiences.**

**St. Mary's was designed by architect William Strickland.**

The tomb was removed from the church for weeks because of the repairs being done at St. Mary's. Ultimately, the church decided that Bishop Richard Pius Miles belonged in the church, but in a new location. Today, he is in a meditation room in a new tomb made of African teakwood that has been resealed.

There are still questions about this tomb that may never be answered. How is it that, if Bishop Miles was the first bishop of Nashville and a prominent man in the community, there was no record of where his remains were? The church has a few theories. Bishop Miles died in 1860—as the Civil War loomed closer to Nashville. Perhaps they did not have time to place a marker or plaque indicating the location of Miles' resting place. Or maybe there was a marker there, and after the war was over it was stolen. The church had been completely looted, so this is a strong possibility. Either way, the members of the church probably always intended to place a monument there, but never got around to it because there was so much work to do not only in the church, but also in post Civil War Nashville. From there the location of the tomb did not get passed down, and from one generation to the next, it simply was lost to history.

The only reason that the general public is even aware of these stories is that from 1969, when the tomb was discovered, until 1973, when the first interviews about these ghost stories were published, the priests in those interviews claimed that the haunting had ceased. They believed now that Bishop Miles' lost tomb had finally been discovered, and that he was now at rest in a marked grave, his soul was at peace. For this reason, the diocese felt they no longer had a secret to hide. They claimed that the sightings had stopped, that the bells had quit ringing, and for this reason felt that the haunting of St. Mary's was over.

But is this true? It's difficult to say with any certainty if Miles truly is at rest. Since 1973, the church has become more conservative about this topic and refuses comment with local reporters, other than to say "No comment." This is of course understandable. If they were to confirm these stories, it would cause another maelstrom of interest, which the church does not desire. If they were to deny these stories, they would essentially be calling Father Cashin and the others who shared their ghost stories liars.

There are still unexplained phenomena occurring at the church today. Hundreds of pictures of ghost 'orbs' have been captured all around the church, especially the tower. Many curious observers, while standing near the entrance to the building, have reported hearing whispered sounds of someone coming from the large, wooden doors. The bells in the tower have been replaced with a more modern mechanical system. They ring every hour on the hour until 8 o'clock at night and do not ring again until the next morning. But late at night, and at all hours of the night, the bells have been known to ring. This always occurs off the hour like 9:17 or 11:42, and sounds like a single bell, not the more melodic ring of the modern bells.

If Bishop Miles is still haunting the church, the public will probably never know. This seems to remain a mystery to all except for the priests at St. Mary's.

# 5

# Lady at the Top of the Stairs

Irish pubs are famous for their ghost stories, and Mulligan's Pub on 2nd Avenue is no different. The building that holds the restaurant and bar dates back to the early 1840s. Over the years there have been dozens of businesses housed there, from saddle shops to doctor's offices, but for whatever reason, many of the businesses closed their doors within a year's time. There since 1990, Mulligan's has certainly lasted the longest. Celtic music, walls covered with signs of Irish colloquialisms, and laughter from the red-nosed regulars huddled around the bar all lend to the ambiance of this local watering hole.

At one point in the 1880s the building was used as a carriage house. The bottom level housed all of the equipment while the upstairs was the living quarters for the caretaker and his wife. It's said that the caretaker's wife took a fatal fall down the stairs. She tumbled from the top of the stairs all the way down to bottom breaking her neck. The caretaker and his wife were known to have had their fair share of fights, but without a witness to her death, it was deemed an accident.

Unresolved murders, or deaths, have historically shown themselves to be the cause of a building's haunting. This indeed seems to be the case at Mulligan's. This ghost often manifests itself in a variety of ways. Cooks in the kitchen area will frequently see pots and pans fly off their hooks crashing to the ground below, or witness a twenty pound bag of coffee fly off the shelf inexplicably.

The main bar area has had a few strange occurrences as well. Late at night, the staff has seen bright flashes of light in the large mirror behind the bar, even though there wasn't a car passing on the street outside.

**Mulligan's Pub is a favorite Irish pub for locals and is haunted by the Lady at the Top of the Stairs.**

One evening, while the bartender and a few servers were clearing away dirty tables, they could hear bottles rattling together downstairs. They all froze where they were working and looked wide-eyed at each other. The bar should have been empty except for the employees. Clearly, it seemed that someone must have hidden inside the restroom or somewhere else in the bar, and had come out to raid the liquor well. The servers planned to corner the would-be thief. A couple went down the backstairs in the kitchen while the others went down the front stairs. As they came down the stairs, the glass continued to clink and rattle. Ready for anything, the servers all spilled into the room, some with clenched fists.

The thief was gone, but this was impossible. Many of the veteran waiters credited the building's ghost as the source of the experience. Some of the newer waiters and waitresses were skeptical at first, but over time became believers as well.

It's the upstairs area that seems to attract the most exciting experiences. There is a narrow staircase near the entrance to

Mulligan's. The hostesses at the restaurant have claimed that the tables at the top of the stairs receive the most complaints. Several times a week a guest will request a new table. This has led the hostesses to believe that somehow the diners are subconsciously aware that something horrible once happened there.

It's at the top of these stairs that the apparition of the woman also appears. She's described as having dark, wavy hair and wearing a cream colored dress. She stands there looking blankly ahead, perhaps reliving the last few seconds of her life. She often appears alone, but sometimes a man is seen standing behind her. This is why people suspect she was murdered. It's as if her murder is being repeated for eternity.

Most everyone who has worked at the bar has seen her at some point. One waitress claimed that the Lady at the Top of the Stairs appears to her in a small porthole shaped mirror. On many occasions this waitress has had an arm full of dishes on her way toward the stairs. Out of the corner of her eye in the plate-sized mirror to her left, she would see this dark haired woman standing behind her. The waitress said this happens about seven out of ten times. Because of the frequency, this waitress makes a point to turn her head away from the mirror before quickly making her way down the stairs.

Another manager claimed to have seen her in the early winter of 2007. The woman appeared in front of her, blocking her way to the staircase. Terrified, she ran right through her toward the stairs. As she rushed by, she did not feel any resistance. Instead she said it was like running through a fog. The manager scurried down the stairs, afraid to look back over her shoulder.

The staff and management are reluctant to talk about her anymore within the walls of the restaurant. They began to notice that the more people acknowledged or spoke of the ghost, the more active she became. Is this because she wants her story known and is in some way trying to communicate with the living? It's difficult to say, but some will only speak of her off hours away from the bar. And some others will not talk about her at all.

# 6

# Ghosts of the Ryman Auditorium

## Captain Tom

The Ryman Auditorium is probably the most historically significant and recognizable building in downtown Nashville. It's nationally known for two main reasons. One, it was the home of the *Grand Ole Opry* from 1943 to 1974. It was during those years that the venue's really legendary performances took place with acts like Patsy Cline, Dolly Parton, Hank Williams, Porter Wagoner, Loretta Lynn, and all of the other top country music stars of the era. During those times, the lines around the block of the Ryman were legendary. Secondly, in polls taken by top performers in entertainment, the Ryman ranks as having the second best acoustics of any music venue in the world, next to the Mormon Gospel Tabernacle. For this reason performers from all over the world continue to perform on this stage, even though the audience capacity is just a few thousand. Like Carnegie Hall, it's on every singer's short list of venues at which they dream of performing. The Ryman's stage has been graced by Bob Hope, Roy Rogers, Mae West, Helen Keller, James Brown, George Carlin, Katharine Hepburn, Bruce Springstein, and countless others.

Although it's known today primarily as an entertainment venue, this was not the original intent. The Ryman actually began as a church. The stained glass at the back of the church is the most obvious sign of the building's original purpose. Today it creates a beautiful effect from outside. During a concert the multicolored windows will flash brightly in rhythm to the music being played within. The result is a visual lightshow like a giant kaleidoscope. The church was built by the most unlikely of men, Captain Tom Ryman.

Tom Ryman was a handsome, wealthy young man, who made most of his fortune in Nashville with his fleet of riverboats and saloons. He was a hard drinker, gambler, and was known to get into the occasional fistfight. He was hardly a model citizen.

A tent revival near the river changed his life. The minister was Sam Jones. He was reknowned around the world and was preaching for several days in town. Lawlessness and saloons ruled the day, and Jones is said to have mentioned Tom Ryman by name in one of his sermons. The story is that Ryman heard of this and became enraged. On May 10, 1885, the drunken Ryman and a few cohorts made their way to the revival with every intention of roughing up this preacher.

Ryman and his friends slipped into the rear of the tent, waiting for an opportunity to either heckle or start a fight. Sam Jones

**The Ryman Auditorium was the home to the *Grand Ole Opry* from 1943 to 1974.**

**Statue of Captain Tom Ryman, whose ghost has been present since 1918.**

spotted him first. The minister called out to Ryman and implored him to change his sinful ways. This public humiliation angered Ryman further, but the turning point came when Jones spoke of his mother. Tom Ryman's mother was a religious woman whom he adored. Sam Jones asked, "What would your mother think of what you've done with your life?" This is said to have silenced Ryman and changed his life.

From that day forward, Ryman vowed to put his sinful ways behind him and transform his life for the better. Ryman banned gambling and liquor on his boats, and he closed down one of his saloons on lower Broadway. Tom Ryman and Sam Jones even became friends

One of the ways that Ryman hoped to make up for his past was to build a church just off of Broadway. At that time, Broadway was known as the Black Bottoms district and was one of the most violent and criminal areas of town. Even the James Gang stayed there and was rumored to have shot a man just a couple of blocks away from where the church was constructed. It was Ryman's hope that he could lure those lawless people into his church because he felt they needed it most. Named the Gospel Tabernacle, which was later renamed the Union Gospel Tabernacle, when it opened in 1892, it was the largest church in Nashville.

Captain Tom Ryman died in 1904, and at his funeral his friend, Sam Jones, presided over 4,000 mourners in attendance at the Union Gospel Tabernacle. It was during the funeral services that Jones recommended that the church be renamed the Ryman Auditorium in his honor. From that point forward, the Ryman ceased being a church, because there were still thousands of dollars owed on the building. It was sold and became an entertainment venue for orchestras, operas, traveling speakers, and political debates.

Fourteen years after Ryman passed, the first ghost stories began to appear. In 1918, a Russian opera called "Carmen" visited Nashville. Bizet's "Carmen" was considered very risqué at least for that day and age. On opening night, patrons repeatedly complained to the Ryman box office that a man was heckling the actors on stage.

The ushers walked down the aisles and could hear a man booing and yelling at the performers. In the darkness, they were unable to find the source of this taunting. This occurred night after night. Heavy equipment would crash backstage during key scenes. The audience could hear feet stomping behind the curtain. The heckler continued to boo and hiss at the actors each night. This ruined the performance for everyone in attendance. Many witnesses who knew Tom Ryman said that it sounded like his voice. This all ceased when "Carmen" left town.

This did not occur again for years, until another controversial musical called "Tobacco Road" played at the Ryman. The heckling started all over again. This has happened at least seven times in the building's history. The common denominator seems to be that whenever a performance that Ryman may have found distasteful is held there, his ghost does anything it can to put a stop to it. Some stories report that during more morally suspect performances, Ryman has been heard reciting Biblical scripture and singing hymns in an attempt to drown out the act on stage.

There has been a variety of country music videos, movies, and live television programs filmed at the Ryman over the years including "The Jimmy Dean Show." A well-documented story involved a television crew from New York. This particular crew had been contracted to come down to Nashville to work on the show. Afterward, they were sharing stories and cavorting with some of the local crewmembers. Those natives told the New Yorkers some of the stories of the building's ghosts, especially the ones involving Tom Ryman. They shared their tales and personal accounts as the visiting production crew rolled their eyes and made rude jokes about their ghost stories. They believed these Southerners to be less educated and superstitious. This of course angered the Southerners, so after a little debate as to the validity of their ghost stories, they dared their northern friends to stay the night themselves and prove them wrong.

Laughing, they accepted the dare and stayed the night inside the Ryman. The Nashville crewmembers left, locking the New York crew inside securely before they left. The remaining crew talked and joked with each other late into the night. Thoughts of spirits and ghosts were the furthest thing from their minds. They were lounging around the pews in the middle of the auditorium, some smoking cigarettes with their feet propped up, when they heard a creak from above. The talking ceased.

They knew they were alone. They had seen the others leave hours ago and had locked the door behind them. From overhead, they could hear the unmistakable sound of a heavy, plodding footstep. Their eyes were huge as they stared at the ceiling above. They heard one step, and then another. With each footfall, they could see little sifts of dust puff out of the cracks in the boards above them. It seemed like an eternity as the sound crossed the floor over their heads. The sound stopped, and the men waited; they were all too scared to even take a breath. No one was laughing now.

They left the Ryman that night before the morning hours, losing the dare. Their stories were published in a New York tabloid weeks later, further solidifying the Ryman's reputation as one of the most haunted buildings in the south.

# Back on Stage

The source for ghost stories is very often tragedy, and country music has certainly seen its fair share. One of country music's larger than life figures is Hank Williams, Sr. He was a legend at the Ryman and probably the most popular performer ever on that stage. He's still the only entertainer to have had six encore performances in the same night there.

Williams was a well-known alcoholic. He struggled with this throughout his short life. Although his wild lifestyle probably contributed to his mystique, it was also a hindrance to his career. He had been given several warnings about his drinking by the *Grand Ole Opry*, but had been unable to put the bottle behind him. He was finally banned from performing at the Opry and the Ryman altogether.

This was devastating to Hank. He was well aware of how important the Opry was to his career, and this blacklisting only hastened his downward spiral with alcohol. Hank Williams was found dead in the backseat of his car on New Year's Day of 1953. He was only 29-years old. He had been seen partying heavily the night before, but there have always been some rumors of foul play in his demise.

Hank Williams had not been able to repair the bridge that had been burned with the *Grand Ole Opry* before he died. People believe that this is why his ghost has attached itself to the Ryman—because he longs to return to the stage that was so important to him.

He has been witnessed on stage, backstage, in dressing rooms, and in the lobby. One of the most recurrent places his apparition appears is the alley behind the Ryman. There have been numerous sightings of Hank exiting the entertainer's entrance to the Ryman into the alley, which connects to Honky Tonk Row. William's specter has been seen crossing the alley to the back entrance of Tootsie's Orchid Lounge.

The original entrance to the Ryman, the site of a number of specters.

**Country Music stars exit through this door...many witnesses have claimed to seen the apparition of Hank Williams here.**

One famous occurrence involved legendary performer Whispering Bill Anderson. A few years after Hank Williams' death, Anderson was booked to play at the *Grand Ole Opry*. The afternoon before that evening's show, Anderson was rehearsing with his guitar. He strummed through a variety of songs while the sound technicians made adjustments at the controls.

Everything progressed routinely, until Anderson began to play the first few bars of one of Hank Williams' favorite songs. The sound blacked out, as did the auditorium lights, stage lights, and even the emergency exit signs. The only light in the room came from the multi-colored stained glass windows at the back of the auditorium. After a few moments, the speakers crackled and the power hummed back to life. The technicians were unable to give a rational explanation for the bizarre power outage, but Anderson insisted that the incident was purely supernatural.

Anderson has famously recounted the incident over the years, claiming that Hank Williams' ghost caused it. This was a positive experience in Anderson's mind. In the years afterward, he felt that the Williams' spirit was connected with him and helped guide Anderson through his musical career.

A security guard also recalled his first meeting with the Ryman's paranormal guests. One early morning, he was strolling down the hall, lost in his own thoughts, when he became aware of the sound of music. He paused with a curious look on his face and looked to his left trying to determine the source.

He was a country music fan, which was the main reason he had initially applied for the job, and recognized the voice as Hank Williams instantly. Could he be hearing music from next door at one of the honky tonks? He didn't think this was likely since he had never been able to hear it before.

What seemed more likely was the idea that he was not alone. It wouldn't be the first time that an over zealous fan had snuck inside to sing on the Ryman stage late at night. Whoever the intruder was had a remarkable resemblance to Williams' voice. Carefully, the guard crept toward the main auditorium. Holding his large flashlight over his shoulder like a baton, he cracked the door open. The dark showroom appeared empty.

The guard turned on his flashlight and swept the light's beam across the room in a cursory search. The music continued. The sound had a muffled, distant quality. He began to search each and every aisle.

After twenty minutes of a futile search, the guard came to believe that there must be another explanation than a trespasser. Maybe someone had placed a radio in the building as a prank. He tried to consider where such a radio might be placed that he could not locate. The biggest problem with finding the source was that it seemed to be nowhere and everywhere at once. In the lobby, the dressing rooms, restrooms, upstairs, and downstairs—the maddening music continued and each time he thought he was close to the source, it always seemed to be just a little further away.

One of the older, veteran employees suggested to him that the spiritual incarnation of Hank Williams had never left the Ryman, and was still performing to an empty auditorium night after night. Although at first this seemed to be an absurd idea to him, over time he secretly began to suspect that the old man had been right.

Over the following weeks, the music would come and go. The other security guards shared similar stories. Some even talked of hearing other Opry greats like Patsy Cline crooning in the building. Could the ghost of Hank Williams still be performing on the stage today?

# The Gray Man

One of the most frequently observed ghosts at the Ryman is known only as the gray man. He appears solely in the balcony of the Ryman. He usually appears when the balcony area is empty and he has it to himself. The person is always described as looking like an older man around seventy years old. He wears a long gray rider's coat and a hat. Many have said he appears to be wearing a Confederate uniform underneath his coat. Sitting alone in the balcony, he has not gone unnoticed. During daytime tours of the Ryman, countless tourists and tour guides have reported seeing this odd man. Security guards and employees have also had sightings of him, but most often it's the performers that have borne witness to the gray man.

During afternoon sound checks when the Ryman is vacant or if the show isn't sold out that evening leaving the balcony empty, many singers have claimed to seen this mysterious man enjoying the performance on the stage below. Often times, a roadie or band manager is sent upstairs to ask the man to leave, but somehow he eludes them each and every time. If left alone, he has been known to sit back and enjoy the performance for extended periods of time.

One of Ryman's museum curators and historians recalled an afternoon during the year before the Ryman reopened following renovations. It was a rainy day, and the curator was walking through the balcony of the Ryman. He noticed a man with a gray coat and hat. Not thinking of ghost stories at all, he believed the man to be one of the city's homeless coming in out of the rain. This had occurred a few times before.

The curator made his way across the balcony and began to descend the steps approaching the row where the homeless man sat. From behind he could see the back of the old man swaddled in his coat and hat, and felt a bit of sympathy for the man he was about to send outside. He watched his feet as he walked down the stairs, always careful not to trip at this height. He considered what approach to use in asking this man to leave. Should he be authoritative or compassionate? It turned out... he didn't have to choose. He looked up from his feet and saw the man was gone.

With his pulse quickening, the curator spun around on his heels looking for the man. He was alone in the balcony. This was impossible. There was no conceivable way to reach the exit in those few seconds. He peered over the edge of the balcony, somewhat relieved to not see his lifeless body sprawled out on the ground below. This logical man stopped to consider the possibilities, and from the back of his mind he remembered coming across accounts of a Confederate haunting the balcony. Not believing in ghosts himself, he had dismissed the stories as over imaginative nonsense. Now he wasn't so sure. He thought of the hat and the gray coat. Was this possible? Over the years he came to believe this to be the only reasonable conclusion.

There has always been some mystery as to the man's identity. Why would a Confederate ghost attach itself to this building? Although the Nashville area has a rich Civil War history, the Ryman itself was not constructed until 1892. This would have been almost thirty years after the war was over.

The answer may be due to an event in 1897. In this year, a reunion was held for Civil War veterans in Nashville. Thousands of veterans traveled from all over the south for the occasion. The large turnout was unexpected and to accommodate the incoming crowds a new balcony was added to the Union Gospel Tabernacle. It was appropriately named the Confederate Gallery. This would explain why an older Confederate ghost might reside in the balcony. Perhaps he died there during the reunion, or perhaps it was so emotionally powerful for him this is why he chooses to stay there for all eternity.

# The Opry's Curse

While the curse of the *Grand Ole Opry* is only indirectly related to its ghost stories, the widely held belief in the curse by Nashvillians and the tremendous amount of coincidences surrounding it makes it worth consideration. The rumors about the Opry curse began to surface in the late 1960s. This is due to the fact that death and tragedy seemed to follow those who performed or worked at the Ryman Auditorium. Year after year, one tragic death seemed to follow another, leading locals to speculate that the Opry was cursed.

Although most people scoffed at the idea, each succeeding death seemed to confirm and validate the curse. These horrible deaths had many similarities; they always occurred to people still very young in age, the demise was often gruesome and violent, and oddly, these deaths involved over thirty-five Opry stars and employees at the Ryman in just over a ten-year period from 1964 to 1974.

The following is a list of many, but not all, of the tragic deaths and near misses of those affiliated with the Opry during this span of time.

• Jim Reeves was a popular performer who died in a plane crash in 1964.

• Ira Louvin, his wife, another couple of friends, and the occupants of another car all died in a head-on collision in 1965.

• Patsy Cline, Cowboy Copas, Randy Hayes, and Hawkshaw Hawkins all died in a famous plane crash in 1965. There is an unconfirmed rumor that Cline had a premonition of her death.

• "Texas Ruby" Fox died of smoke inhalation in a terrible fire that consumed her home.

• Stringbean Akeman (*Hee Haw* comedian) and his wife were murdered during a robbery at their home in 1963.

• Jimmy Widener, who performed with Hank Snow, and his girlfriend were murdered in 1973.

• Hank Williams, Jr. fell from a Montana mountain in 1975, resulting in years of surgery and therapy. This left him physically scarred for life.

In 1974 the Opry moved to a new location at Opryland. The future of the Ryman was in doubt, as there was movement to demolish the building and construct corporate offices. Fortunately the auditorium was spared; years later it was renovated and reopened, saving an important, historic treasure. Some have speculated that the negative publicity of the Opry curse was a factor in the desire to destroy the building. Could this have been an attempt to put the persistent ghost and curse talk to rest by corporate executives motivated more by a bottom line than the preservation of a historic landmark? This question may never be answered.

In fact only more questions seem to be raised. Many say that because a large part of the original stage was moved to the new location at Opryland, by doing so they have taken the curse and haunting with them. Tragedy does still seem to follow the Opry today, and there have been sporadic reports of unexplained phenomena at the new Opry house. It appears that if it was anyone's motivation to leave the curse behind, then that effort may have been in vain.

# 7

# Tootsie's Orchid Lounge

On Broadway between 4th and 5th Avenues is the location of the city's most famous honky tonk. Because they are located so close to the Ryman Auditorium, these dive bars became amazing venues for up and coming country stars. Countless future Country Music Hall of Fame musicians cut their teeth at these often-rowdy clubs. Today, these bars are as much historic sites as they are entertaining watering holes. Arguably the most famous of which is Tootsie's Orchid Lounge. The building is over a century old, and according to the owner, at one time in the late 1800s was one of the many downtown brothels. During the country music boom of the 1950s, the two-story, brick building was known as Mom's Place and was a favorite bar of Hank Williams. He often performed on stage and was known to have a cocktail or two as well. Many claim to have seen Hank's apparition perform on stage, as well as at the bar having a drink.

Tootsie Bess purchased the nightclub in 1960. The building required a makeover and an investment of a lot of money, but Tootsie knew she had a goldmine, due to the alley connecting it to the back door of the Ryman.

One of her first orders of business was to have the building painted. The story is that Tootsie ordered the paint herself, accidentally writing down the wrong serial number for the color. The painters picked up the paint cans from the store and began their work. After just a few brush strokes it became clear to them that this building would not look like the other buildings on Broadway. The paint's color was an unusual blend of pink and purple. Never suspecting the mistake, the workers painted the exterior of the tavern from top to bottom.

**The most famous of all the honky tonks, Tootsie's Orchid Lounge is said to be looked after by the former owner, Tootsie Bess.**

When Tootsie came down to view her newly painted investment, she looked at the building and stood in silence for several minutes. How would most people react? She would have been justified in being angry with either herself or even the painters for not questioning the strangeness of color. No one would have blamed her for repainting the entire club either, so that it would match the other clubs on the block.

Instead, she saw the positive, "Well, at least my club will stand out from the rest." She even named the bar The Orchid Lounge because of the building's color. The club was a success and became a virtual "green room" for the *Grand Ole Opry* performers next door.

The club was a hangout for countless performers including Hank Cochran, Mel Tillis, Waylon Jennings, Patsy Cline, Faron Young, Charlie Pride, Webb Pierce, and Roger Miller. Over one hundred recorded songs are said to have been written there. Tootsie often allowed up and comers to live and perform there in exchange for cleaning up after hours. Both Willie Nelson and Kris Kristofferson lived in the apartment there early in their careers. Willie Nelson famously sold a song called "Crazy" to Patsy Cline that he wrote while living at Tootsie's

Tootsie Bess herself is a country music icon and has been immortalized in several country songs. She was beloved by her performers. Charlie Pride was a little concerned for Tootsie's safety. Even though she was a brassy, headstrong woman, Pride worried that some of the inebriated patrons might harm her. She expressed her ability to take care of herself, but Pride was not satisfied. Legend is that he gave her a golden hatpin and said, "If any of those men get out of line, I want you to stick them with this." Tootsie kept the hatpin, and in fact used it for the next twenty years. Anytime the drunks got out of line, she would give them a jab in the ribs with her hatpin. If it was closing time and the crowd wouldn't leave after last call, she'd start poking them with her pin, herding the regulars out the door. The pin was very much a symbol of Tootsie Bess herself.

Tootsie's funeral was attended by Connie Smith, Faron Young, Roy Acuff, and Tom T. Hall. She was buried in an orchid gown, in an orchid coffin, and with a single orchid placed in her hand.

She is still believed to be looking over her Orchid Lounge. There have been several stories since her passing that when a customer gets loud or rowdy, they sometimes yelp in surprise as if being stuck in the back by something. They of course spin around to confront the aggressor, but no one is there. This usually diffuses the situation, leaving the drunk bewildered by what happened. It appears to the current staff of Tootsie's, that even in death, she has kept her sense of humor.

# 8

## Poltergeists

### 918 Petway

I n late April of 1966, a young reporter answered the phone at his desk. Little did he know that the woman on the other end of the line would lead him on a fantastic trail that would not only change his preconceptions about the spirit realm, but she would also give him a front-page story.

The woman who contacted this reporter was Mrs. J. R. Mansfield. She began, "I'm so sorry to bother you. I just didn't know whom else to call. I called the gas company, the police, but no one will help me."

Her frustration was apparent, even over the phone. Although the reporter assumed that the woman was probably about to share some mundane story about her heating bill or an irritating neighbor, he politely offered, "Well, I'd be happy to help, if I can." He grabbed a pen and a worn notepad. "Your name Miss...?"

"Mrs. J. R. Mansfield. I live at 918 Petway in East Nashville." The area was familiar to him. The area held some of the city's historic homes.

"You mentioned the police. Was there a crime of some kind?" he asked, almost hopefully.

"No," she said and then reconsidered, "I mean, possibly. I'm not certain." Then Mrs. Mansfield posed a question of her own, "Could I ask, did you have any reports of an earthquake or maybe an explosion?"

The reporter answered, "Well, certainly no earthquakes. But explosions? Do you mean like fireworks?" He imagined young boys firing off firecrackers outside this woman's window, and then running and laughing as she burst out the door.

"No, No. This was an *explosion*," she said drawing out the word for emphasis. "It shook my whole house."

"I see." Again he checked his memory for possibilities. Had there been any buildings set for demolition? He didn't think so. "Was the sound nearby?"

"There was no sound. That's why I thought maybe it was an earthquake. I was sitting in my living room watching television. The whole house trembled. Not like a large truck driving by or an airplane over the house. It was like a dynamite blast without noise." The impact of this event on her was evident in the tone of her voice. She sounded both like a woman afraid and confident at the same time.

She went on to describe how in those few seconds, the candlesticks and porcelain figurines rattled wildly on their shelves. The TV antenna swung sporadically, causing the rabbit ears to spin and fall to the ground. The glass covering a picture over her fireplace mantel cracked like breaking ice on a frozen pond before crashing to the floor below. The silver shards bounced and danced in a million pieces. Without realizing she was doing it, Mrs. Mansfield screamed and stood from her chair with arms outstretched as if to keep balance.

The force of the blast made her feel as if a fault line had opened beneath her and was going to swallow up her and her home in an instant.

But then... it stopped.

The room was again still, and Mrs. Mansfield stood waiting with broken glass and overturned lamps at her feet. She realized she was screaming and stopped. The only sound was the buzz from the black and white television, which due to the fallen antenna only displayed the common white snow of a lost signal.

When she felt safe (or at least *safer*), she checked the rest of the home. Apparently, the entire house had been affected. Kitchen cabinets stood open, many of which had spilled out their contents of canned foods and bottles all over the countertops. Picture frames, wall calendars, and prints all over the house that had been so carefully placed before by the proud homeowner, now were all in complete disarray. Putting everything back in its appropriate place, as Mrs. Mansfield would later learn, would take her weeks.

When Mrs. Mansfield asked her neighbors about the tremor, they all responded with looks of bewilderment and a shrug of their shoulders. "What earthquake?"

Determined to solve this mystery, she called the police. They seemed to have no knowledge of any explosions, earthquakes, bombs, underground mining, or construction blasting that might have caused this. "We'll look into it," which Mrs. Mansfield, probably accurately, took to mean, "We've got more important things to do, like locate lost pets and protect the city from its growing number of reckless jaywalkers, but if it makes you feel better to imagine a team of Nashville's Finest working late hours on one crazy bird's "earthquake" phenomena, then I'll gladly say, 'we'll look into it.' Don't call us. We'll call you."

She began to feel like no one was taking her seriously, and suspected that some of the neighbors might even be snickering behind her back and making fun of a woman suffering the early stages of dementia. A concerned friend offered a logical explanation, "Maybe it's your furnace. If it's about to blow, you might want to check it out. For your own safety."

This sounded plausible to her, and she promptly had the gas company out to the house. An hour or so later, the serviceman returned without any answers. "Call us if you have anymore trouble." Again, Mrs. Mansfield detected a hint of insincerity in this man's voice like the others. Her last resort was the press.

The reporter was sympathetic to the woman, but more importantly, he believed her. He promised her, "I'm going to look into this and call you if I find anything." Over the phone, he grimaced to himself, realizing he probably sounded like everyone else that had offered her empty promises.

If she was disappointed, she at least didn't seem to be over the phone, "Thank you for your time."

He kept his word and checked out the story and possible causes. He quickly ruled out the obvious possibilities. During a conversation about this woman's inexplicable house tremor with another reporter, a new possibility was offered. "You know, this kind of reminds me of a story we ran three or four years ago about a poltergeist on 9th Avenue."

The reporter paused with his cup of coffee halfway to his lips. He looked at the other man, not taking a drink, but setting the mug carefully back on his desk. "Poltergeist?" he asked.

"Yeah, you know, a ghost. Haunted houses. That kind of thing," he answered looking back at the reporter. He stiffened up a bit, "Hey, I didn't write the story." He seemed almost defensive.

The other man mistook his enthusiasm for skepticism. Regardless, the wheels in his mind were turning already.

He had his story... A *GHOST* story.

# 1627 9th Avenue

The reporter investigated and uncovered a supernatural phenomenon that had occurred in 1962. The events had taken place at 1627 9th Avenue in Nashville, just a few miles from Mrs. Mansfield's home. The house was better known as the Hawkins House. John Hawkins owned it and lived there with his family. According to reports, they began having strange activity in the home almost immediately upon moving in.

At first the experiences were more curious than terrifying. Dressed in a bathrobe, Hawkins made his way down the hall towards the bathroom. He heard footsteps behind him. He turned back expecting to see one of his children, but the hall was empty.

On another occasion, the family was gathered around the dining table for dinner; the parents shared news of the day while the children eagerly waited for permission to leave and resume their games. Unexpectedly, a peppershaker slid four or five inches across the table. The talking stopped immediately. Everyone looked at each other wide eyed and surprised, almost asking for an explanation from the others with their eyes. John Hawkins made an uncomfortable and puzzled laugh, and the others followed suit. His wife said in disbelief, "Well, I've never..." Mrs. Hawkins looked at her husband suspiciously, "John, did you...was this a trick?"

John raised his hands quickly with a grin, "No, no not me. I promise." She held her stare at Mr. Hawkins like a poker player trying to crack his opponent's bluff. After a moment she conceded, "Fine. I believe you." She paused and considered, "It's strange though. How could it have…" her voice trailed off.

"I know," John offered, as perplexed as his wife, "it's very funny."

Their experiences were **NOT** funny for long.

Over the following weeks they all individually experienced these types of activity. On one night, a hairbrush flew out of his wife's hand halfway across the room, as if slapped by an invisible force. The footsteps continued. The children's toys would disappear for days and then mysteriously return, sitting in the middle of their bed when they got home from school. Privately, they each began to suspect dark forces, but didn't share their fears with each other. They probably could have continued to live with these types of events, but not the ones that followed.

Late one night, John Hawkins was awakened by a knocking sound. *Knock. Knock. Knock.* The sound continued not quite in rhythm.

"John? What is that sound?" his wife mumbled half asleep. She was a sound sleeper.

"I don't know." He tried to go back to sleep, but the sound continued even louder. *Knock. Knock.* Was someone at the door? *Knock. Knock. Knock. Knock. Knock.* Maybe it was a branch blowing against the house?

"John, would you please…?" his wife started, but John cut her off. "I'll take care of it. Go back to sleep," he offered, knowing that would be difficult until he found what was causing this noise. As deep a sleeper as she was, he knew no one could rest with this sound that seemed to be getting louder. John swung his legs off of his bed into his carefully placed slippers on the floor. He grabbed his robe and walked toward the door. He hoped to fix the problem and get back to bed quickly so that the children wouldn't wake up.

Originally the sound seemed to be coming from just outside of his bedroom, but was now resonating from the living room. He stopped to grab a flashlight from the hall closet and made his way toward the sound. *KNOCK. KNOCK. KNOCK.* He turned a table lamp on. The sound was certainly louder, and he now thought he heard the children stirring upstairs. "Damn," he cursed under his breath anticipating a long night of putting the kids back in bed.

With each pounding beat, John watched—the sound seemed to move across the wall into the kitchen. He followed.

***KNOCK. KNOCK. KNOCK. KNOCK.***

He considered the possibilities. A rodent trapped in the walls? Expanding water pipes? Nothing seemed to fit, and the banging thump started to make it difficult to think. He opened the front door to see if maybe a branch was the culprit as he originally thought. He turned on the flashlight and walked around the front of the house.

***KNOCK. KNOCK. KNOCK. KNOCK. KNOCK. KNOCK.***

There was not even a slight breeze outside. He used the beam from the flashlight to scan the roof of the house expecting any moment for the light to reveal some kind of snarling night creature. He determined that there was nothing unusual about the house, other than the noise. He turned to go back inside, almost plowing right into his wife. One of her hands was outstretched, as if she were trying to tap his shoulder, while the other was clutched at her chest holding her robe together.

He nearly screamed.

"I'm sorry I scared you. I was calling out to you. I suppose you couldn't hear over this noise."

John smiled at himself, "It's all right."

His wife looked around their house, "What's happening to our home?" He didn't have an answer.

Unfortunately, over the following weeks, the noise continued. This didn't happen every night or in any discernable pattern. Sometimes the hammering sound would occur for several days in a row. It could last for minutes or unbelievably hours. There were times that they were given a reprieve for a week or so, allowing them the false hope that it was over, and then as before the first few unmistakable beats would start up again. This would always cause John and his wife to cringe. The whole experience was like a relentless migraine.

Like Mrs. Mansfield, they sought solutions through a variety of sources. Policemen, electricians, plumbers, and gas service personnel were all unable to pinpoint the problem. Unlike Mrs. Mansfield, the Hawkins family sought council from a less traditional source. They called upon the service of a parapsychologist.

The parapsychologist made a thorough examination of the home. After days of analysis and interviews with the family, he concluded that the home exhibited the classic signs of a poltergeist. The word *poltergeist* is German for "noisy ghost," which this one certainly was. The owner before the Hawkins family had been a fireman. The firefighter had died tragically on the job in a fire at a manufacturing company in 1937. By the parapsychologist's estimation, this was most likely the root of the Hawkins' troubles.

In some ways this was satisfying to have found an answer, but in many ways it just opened up a whole new set of challenges. The parapsychologist documented his findings, and the local paper ran the story shortly afterward in October of 1962. Enthused locals came from all around the state to see this building for themselves. John Hawkins would often find strangers standing in his yard photographing his house or carrying lit candles offering up bizarre chants in attempts to conjure up the dead. The knocking sounds at night had now been joined by another knocking at his door. This only made the situation less tolerable.

Eventually, the interest tapered off and less people visited the home. After this experience, the Hawkins family did not share their stories with the public, probably afraid of more attention. It's possible that they may have had some sort of exorcism to try and remove the spirit, but this is unknown.

The young reporter turned in his ghost story to his editor, which not only described Mrs. Mansfield's "silent explosion," but also recalled the events at the Hawkins' home as reported in 1962. The story made the front page. He was unsure if this would please Mrs. Mansfield or not. This may have given her the answers she sought. Perhaps this would lead her on a journey to discover the history of her home, and maybe she would find what had caused her home to shake at its foundation. She might even find a way to prevent it from happening again.

It was his hope that at least this explanation would allow her mind to be at rest, even if the spirit in her home was not.

# 9

# Adelicia Acklen

One of Nashville's most controversial, historic figures is Adelicia Acklen. At her peak, the fair-skinned, dark-haired belle was said to be one of the wealthiest and powerful women in the South. Many have viewed her as having admirable qualities for her ability to come out of the Civil War not only financially secure, but also even *wealthier* than before. Whereas her supporters have described her as having guile, resolve, and survivor instincts, her detractors have painted her as manipulative, immoral, and selfish. As is often the case with historic figures that are both adored by some and criticized by others, the truth is more gray than black or white. Her strengths or flaws are more dependent upon one's point of view.

Adelicia Hayes was born into a prominent Nashville family in 1817. Adelicia's first marriage was to a wealthy businessman named Isaac Franklin. Immediately eyebrows were raised due to the disparity in age. She was twenty-two years old and he was nearly fifty. Adelicia gave birth to four beloved children and appeared to be happy in her marriage. They owned several cotton plantations in Louisiana, a large farm in Tennessee, and over 750 slaves. She enjoyed the comforts of her life, but as the world has a habit of proving time and time again, no one is impervious to tragedy. Each of her four children died before the age of eleven and her husband also passed in their seventh year of marriage.

After a period of mourning, at the age of thirty-two, Adelicia married Joseph Acklen, another man of financial means. Joseph Acklen was a lawyer from Alabama. He agreed to a prenuptial agreement with Adelicia, which was very rare for that period of time. This protected her fortune in the event of a divorce. Together they had six children, including twins.

**Adelicia Acklen was a real life Scarlet O'Hara.
Her mansion is rumored to be haunted by her ghost.**

In 1850, they constructed Belmont Mansion. The mansion was 20,000 square feet. It was built in the style of an Italian villa and was surrounded by legendary gardens. As Adelicia's wealth grew, so did the grandeur of the estate itself. The mansion was decorated with rare artwork, Venetian glass, and statues from Europe. The home boasted a menagerie and even a zoo. Adelicia was especially fond of her lavish, circular gardens and found ways to expand and enhance them each year. The property held an artificial lake and a refinery, so that they could produce their own gas for lighting. At the time, Nashville did not have a public park, so Adelicia opened up her vast gardens to the people. This act helped her relationship and image with the other citizens of Nashville. Built for entertaining, Belmont Mansion even held a bowling alley with a billiards parlor. Adelicia Acklen was hardly

**Adelicia's taste for statues of Greek gods and animals is part of the reason that students at Belmont University speculate that she had ties to the occult.**

modest with her spending, which opened her up to scrutiny by some of the city's more conservative citizens.

The majority of the South's elite adored Adelicia, and her galas, balls, and cotillions soon became legendary. The events were usually held in her elaborate gardens. She would decorate the estate with different themes, often lighting the garden with Japanese lanterns and exotic décor. Adelicia *always* held her parties on the nights of a full moon. The events never began until eleven o'clock or later. Adelicia always played her part as hostess, greeting and chatting with the Old South's most powerful moguls. Like one of the constantly moving bees in her flower garden, she would visit each couple with charm and humor briefly before excusing herself to visit another guest. She would continue this social dance all evening, very much enjoying the attention and power she felt.

It's easy to imagine what it must have been like to be at the base of the mansion's hill, seeing the faint glow of the lanterns over the trees and hearing the festive music and laughter rolling down the slopes of the hill. Was this received by neighbors with jealousy? Did the most pious of Nashville's citizenry believe her to be decadent and proud? Probably.

Adelicia Acklen's life of splendor and high society may have made the tragedies of her first marriage seem a lifetime away. Her lifestyle may have even helped keep the grief at bay. If this new marriage and life were some kind of escape for her pain, it would soon be cruelly ripped away from her again. Adelicia gave birth to twins, Corinne and Laura, each of whom died of scarlet fever within days of each other. All of the torment that had been barely held in check now came back in force. The loss of the twins is said to have been the most difficult of all her life.

According to historic accounts, after their deaths, Adelicia would enter the twins' bedroom at the mansion. Untouched after the funerals, she would walk aimlessly through the room that was still full of the children's carefully chosen clothing and their little beds lined with exquisite dolls adorned in dresses more expensive than most of Nashville's citizens. She would pass by the furniture running her fingers absently over the rails of each piece as she passed. Her eyes were glassy and red from the weeks of mourning, and her mind was in another place and time trying to find her way through the misery.

She later told friends that at times she believed she could hear the twins laughing in the way that only the world's most innocent can. Adelicia would spin around from whichever window she had been blankly staring at, her heart foolishly full of hope. The empty room behind her would always crush this brief moment of optimism, leaving her to wonder what she could have done to deserve this fate. Was Adelicia experiencing the ghosts of her precious children, or was this a cruel trick of her mind trying desperately to bring her twins back to life?

It's impossible for most to understand what she must have felt during this time, and most mothers under similar circumstances would have no doubt entered a tail-spin of depression and withdrawal from which they most likely would not have recovered. But Adelicia was, in a word, a survivor. Throughout her life, whenever life seemed to throw impossible tragedy or obstacles at her feet, she always seemed to come through stronger. To her critics, this makes her a cold person. How could this widow, who had lost her children to death, continue to host these wild parties and flaunt her wealth about town? Others view her as heroic in her ability to persevere.

A great example of the woman's tenacity occurred during the Civil War. Joseph Acklen felt the call to fight for the Confederacy. He died in battle, leaving Adelicia twice widowed. For plantation owners in the war, this was a difficult time. Most lost everything. Many of the plantations were burned to the ground or seized and used by Union armies for hospitals or their own living quarters.

Aware of the impending doom facing her estate and fortune, Adelicia Acklen traveled to Louisiana. She had cotton crops there that were an enormous part of her income. The Confederates had seized her 2,800 bales of cotton and were considering burning them, so that the Union army wouldn't obtain them. Adelicia made plans to secretly travel to Louisiana to save her cotton and her fortune. The hundreds of miles of travel from Tennessee to Louisiana opened her eyes to the destruction the war had caused. She witnessed countless dead soldiers, the charred shells of previously grand homes, and passed many bloodied and bandaged soldiers on the roadside that were traveling to unknown destinations. The journey was undoubtedly treacherous, especially so for a woman of Adelicia's beauty.

All of those years spent flirting and socializing with the country's most powerful men at her late night celebrations had helped her hone skills that later proved to be priceless. Using her charm and manipulative abilities, she arranged to have her cotton crop spared by both the Union and Confederates. With the duplicitous guile of Rhett Butler and the enchanting abilities of Scarlet O'Hara, she worked both sides of the war to her advantage with perfection. Using her charismatic skills, she convinced the Confederates to spare the cotton and she later contracted a Yankee wagon train to transport her cotton to a Union port in New Orleans, but the obvious problem emerged. How could she send this Union wagon train safely through the South without being robbed by a group of Rebels? Remarkably, through her talents of persuasion she arranged for a group of Rebel soldiers to escort and secure her goods on the long journey to New Orleans. Neither side was ever aware that she had made deals with the other. The cotton safely arrived in New Orleans and it was sold to a family in London. She cleared nearly one million dollars thanks to her fearless cunning.

After the Civil War, whereas nearly all of the other elite were financially devastated, Adelicia emerged even wealthier than before.

Adelicia was married a third time, and the wedding was held at the Belmont Mansion. The wedding and festivities, of course, was one for the ages.

Adelicia sold the home in 1887 and moved to Washington, D.C. She died that same year. Her remains were returned to Nashville, where she was buried.

The Belmont Mansion became part of an all-girl's school. With an emphasis on the arts, it has helped produce such well-known entertainers as Mary Martin and Minnie Pearl (Sara Ophelia Cannon). In the 1950s it became Belmont College (under the Southern Baptist Convention), which was a four-year college. Today it's known as Belmont University and has a great reputation, especially in areas of the arts.

**Adelicia Acklen's tomb is one of the most interesting tombs in Mt. Olivet Cemetery.**

The university's buildings have been erected all about the hill of the grand estate, but Belmont Mansion still remains the centerpiece of the campus. It has been well preserved and is as grand as ever.

According to sources, Adelicia Acklen has never truly left her home. Her ghost has been witnessed for decades by faculty and students past and present. While Belmont University officials have not always promoted the ghost stories (probably because of the religious implications), the stories persist through graduates and former teachers. Many a late night study session has turned into a round of sharing ghost legends and rumors.

Her haunting of the building is well accepted by most, but it's the 'why' that has been debated. Some believe that Adelicia is still roaming her home because, in her greed, she's not willing to let go of her earthly possessions. Others suspect that her spirit is still restless because of the loss of her children and that she was never able to overcome her grief. Regardless, there are plenty that support the notion that she continues to walk the palatial halls of Belmont Mansion.

Forever the socialite, Adelicia's ghost is most often encountered during festive times of the year. She especially makes her presence known during Christmas. One of the university's best traditions is the Yuletide Hanging of the Green ceremony each year before Christmas. A massive tree is mounted in the main hallway. During the highly anticipated ceremony, a chorus descends the stairs dressed in top hats and nineteenth century-style costumes. Each member carries a lit candle, and they carefully space themselves on the staircase as their carols resonate through the halls.

This type of elaborate event and ceremony would have no doubt appealed to Adelicia's tastes. During the days of preparation, countless students have claimed to hear her. One such evening in the Ladies' Sitting Room, students were busy preparing ribbons, pulling ornaments from last year's boxes, and unraveling garland with their supplies sprawled out on long tables. From above they heard footsteps crossing the floor. The conversation stopped. The students looked at each other as the footsteps made their way across the ceiling, stopped for a moment, and then came back in the direction that it had started. It was almost as if someone was pacing the floor.

The students took a mental roll of everyone in the Ladies Sitting Room and realized that everyone was accounted for. Late at night, the doors were locked leaving only the students who were preparing for the upcoming festivities inside.

"Did you hear that?" one of the girls asked, knowing the others had. A few nodded a silent confirmation.

The footsteps started up again. "Maybe we should go look," one of the boys said more as a question than a statement. A little frightened, but mostly curious, they went upstairs to investigate. They could each feel the adrenaline and nervous energy of the moment as they approached the door. They realized that the room the sound had been coming from was the former master bedroom of Adelicia Acklen.

The students hesitated at the door for a brief instant. Finally, one of the young men in the group stepped from behind and boldly approached the door. He turned the knob and opened the door looking back briefly with an expression that said, "I'll do it since no one else will." He strode inside with everyone following close behind.

The room was empty and still, except for the slight movement of the curtains. This was probably caused by an air duct or a breeze from outside, but maybe…

The same young man who had opened the door also made his way toward the window, obviously thinking along the same lines as the others. He grabbed the curtain as if to pull it back and paused a beat, building up the tension from the others. Everyone seemed to be holding their breaths. He pulled back on the drapes revealing nothing but the bare trees outside. Relieved to a certain extent, they made their way back downstairs to their work.

They soon forgot about the footsteps and were back to the decorations, gossiping, and joking as they worked. It was not long before the footsteps returned. This time, no one went upstairs to check. They told each other it was because there was no point. They had, after all, checked fruitlessly once before. But secretly, they knew it was because they didn't want to discover what they might find.

They each worked quickly and completed their preparations a little bit faster than they normally would have.

Others have confirmed this story in the years since. The footsteps are most often heard from the Ladies Sitting Room, although they have been heard in a few other areas of the mansion as well. Another male student reported not hearing Adelicia, but feeling her presence. On the staircase near her bedroom, he said he felt like someone brushed by him, and then again a few minutes later. Chilled by the encounter, he later believed it to be the spirit of Adelicia.

There are also instances of her essence being captured on film; the former director, Tirri Parker, related one such story. The director said that on one occasion, while taking a tour of the mansion, he took a picture of his friends near a mirror in the home. To his amazement, there was an extra person in his photograph. Near the mirror appeared the image of a woman who looked very similar to Adelicia Acklen.

Another similar experience involved a legend surrounding the mantle clock in the home. It was said that on the day and at the precise moment that Joseph Acklen was slain in battle, the clock on the mantle quit working. Superstition among the house servants of that day was that if the clock was placed in Joseph's personal sitting room, it would start ticking again as if it were brand new.

This legend and others surrounding Belmont Mansion are well known to the students. One undergraduate was taking photos of the mansion for the next year's annual. He noticed the clock and recalled the myth he had heard about as a freshman. Impulsively, he hung the camera around his neck and made his way towards the mantle. His eyes darted back and forth briefly; for a second he wondered what kind of reprimand he might receive for touching the clock. He figured the risk to be low and lifted the clock off the mantle.

It was lighter than he would have guessed, and he made his way toward Joseph's sitting room. He would have looked like some kind of storefront looter if anyone passed by, but they didn't. The photographer carefully placed the clock on the mantle. He stepped back from it to see if it was centered.

What happened next was shocking. Although he knew a little of the legend, he never *actually* expected the minute hand to move, but it did. The minute hand moved one space landing at two minutes past one. There was almost a small whine, as if the clock was taking in a breath, and then the ticking started. The surprising ticking sound seemed very loud to him, and in his brief panic he wondered if someone else, a curious professor perhaps, might come in to find this sophomore rearranging furniture.

This was, of course, not possible. The sound was faint...only exaggerated in his mind by his surprise. Before he knew it, he was holding up his camera and snapping away. He felt a strange buzz in the air, unsure at the time if it was his own adrenaline or something else. After a roll was gone, he lowered the camera and looked back at the clock, which now said that it was 2:04. In an instant, it struck him. He held out his left arm to view his wristwatch.

**2:04.**

He could feel his knees buckle a bit. It seemed to him that the stories were true, but before he could consider any further, he heard footsteps echoing down the hall. He rushed over to the mantle and lifted the clock. The ticking stopped immediately. Maybe his moving the clock had jarred something free, allowing it to work again for a few brief minutes. Or, then again, maybe not.

It occurred to him to put the clock back on the mantle to see if it would start up again, but he knew he didn't have that much time. He thought he could hear voices.

He placed the clock back on its original mantle, and within seconds the voices that he had heard entered the room. It was a group of incoming freshmen being led on the tour by a University representative. The group's guide was speaking to the group, walking backward so she could face them. The photographer passed them going the opposite direction. The group looked at him curiously. Even the confident sounding guide seemed to pause a moment when she saw him. On his way out he passed by a mirror, and upon seeing himself there, he realized why. His cheeks were bright red, which always happened when he was nervous or excited, and there were beads of sweat dripping down his face.

He was glad to be out of the house and was anxious to see how his pictures would turn out. He developed the pictures in a campus lab that night. As the first photograph began to come to life, even under the red lights of the dark room, he knew something was not right. The clock began to appear, but so did someone else. The unmistakable shape of a human emerged. It soon became clear that it was a woman, although she wore what looked like a cloak. He fell back a step, steadying his hand on the wall. If he could have seen himself right then, he knew his cheeks would have been embarrassingly red.

No one else was there when he took the picture. He was positive of that. He shared the picture with others, and soon the picture was well known around campus.

There are those that believe that Adelicia is still hosting her festive engagements. A woman named Mrs. Moore used to live adjacent to the mansion as part of her financial compensation for working for the university. Over the years she complained that the ghosts kept her awake on many nights. The noises were so frustrating for her that she eventually moved out for good.

A similar experience involved the Historic Belmont Auxiliary. Many of the members stayed in guest rooms during the restoration. Tools and equipment kept disappearing from the house. This led to finger-pointing and suspicion amongst the laborers. But at night, some of them reported hearing what sounded like a party. They could hear the clinking of glasses, distant laughter, and what sounded like hoop skirts dragging the ground. These noises all came from the direction of the ballroom. Upon entry, the ballroom always proved to be vacant. It appears that some of the party's guests have had such a wonderful time that they refuse to leave.

Another eyewitness account came from a former student at Belmont University. She claimed that among the student body, Adelicia's ghost stories were well known and discussed. Some of the students believed that Adelicia had interests in the occult. This was due to some of the décor about the property. Goat heads and chalices could be found in the gazebos. Some of the artwork and statues of animals raised questions about her in the eyes of many of the religiously conservative students.

One early morning, at around 2 a.m., the witness and two of her friends accessed the mansion. She claimed to have known of the ghost story, but her interest that night more involved the rumors of Adelicia's occult ties. They hoped to discover something that would indicate this. With flashlights in hand, they wandered about the bottom floor. There wasn't anything of much interest there, so they ventured to the second floor.

This level was mostly used as office space and storage with the exception of Adelicia's bedroom and the children's room. The trio entered the master bedroom first. The coldness of the room was striking. The witness looked around the room for an open window or for air blowing cold air through a vent, but was unable to find either. Although it seemed a little strange, neither she nor her friends thought too much about it.

They next went into the children's room. Here she saw a designed opening in the wall. The story was that during Adelicia's parties the children would sneak out of bed and perch themselves there, craning their necks in an effort to watch the guests below.

The witness leaned out over the opening to see for herself. Below she could see the elegant stairs winding down to the hall below. She pulled back and started to leave, but for a reason she could not later explain, she went back.

This time the stairs were not empty. A woman in a ballroom gown was standing below. Terrified, she ran back to the others. She grabbed one of the boys around his upper arm, spinning him around, "We've got to go. Now!" Confused, they followed her out of the house.

Two years later, she rarely thought about the experience anymore, but one late afternoon as the sun was settling behind the trees on the west side of campus, she passed by Belmont Mansion with a backpack slung over one shoulder. She casually glanced up at the building, and saw a woman looking back at her through the window. She could not make out the lady's facial features, but felt certain it was *HER*. It was not nearly as terrifying this time as the last, as she stood below the window looking back at her. In a strange way, it was even calming, watching her stand there in her window.

There have been other sightings of a woman walking the grounds, sometimes witnessed by students in late night "cram" sessions or even by faculty. Individually, the stories are not always taken seriously by officials, but together they form a pattern of activity that leads to the conclusion, that Adelicia Acklen is just as resilient in death as she was in life.

# 10

# Death to Free Speech

One of the city's most scandalous and vicious events that has ever occurred is largely unknown to most of today's Nashvillians. In its time, though, it was a shocking, tragic ordeal. Edward Ward Carmack was from Sumner County just north of Nashville. In 1858, he was born to a low-income family, but was soon recognized by his teachers for his brilliance. He attended the prestigious Webb School. Carmack always had a fiery temper and left the school over a minor disagreement with another student about religion. Even without completing his formal education, he taught himself law and became a well-respected lawyer in Columbia, Tennessee.

His passion and talent did not go unnoticed by his peers. It was not long before he was elected to the Tennessee State legislature. He later served in the U.S. House of Representatives and in the Senate. His rise to power had been fast and seemingly limitless. In 1907, at the Democratic convention, his name was on a short list of candidates for the Presidential nomination.

What an impressive level of accomplishments he had achieved, from poverty and out of school to rumors of a presidential nomination. Some may have faltered at the opportunity, but Carmack felt the Presidency to be his destiny. After the Democratic convention, in a race for Tennessee's governorship, Carmack lost the Democratic nomination to Malcolm Patterson. The disappointment was devastating to Carmack. Any chance of a presidential nomination was nearly impossible now. How could he expect to carry a nation's vote when he was unable to carry the party in his own state?

A man of many talents, Carmack had worked as editor-in-chief of the *Memphis Commercial Appeal* and the *Nashville Democrat*. After

Statue of Edward Carmack. Slain for his relentless editorials, many have championed him a martyr for free speech.

the loss to Patterson, Carmack accepted the same position with the *Nashville Tennessean*. A man of strong opinions and convictions, the editorials by Carmack were widely read and a popular section of the paper.

One of the hot button topics of the day was the issue of prohibition. Newly elected Governor Patterson was in support of legal alcohol consumption and sales, while Carmack viewed the nearly one hundred saloons in the downtown area to be a blemish on the city. Carmack used the editorials to promote his support of prohibition and almost daily singled out Governor Patterson. Cynics say that Carmack only attacked Patterson out of jealousy and bitterness, but supporters of Carmack view him as a man of strong beliefs and a champion of free speech.

It can be difficult to imagine an age before cable news information channels, Internet, local televised news, and a plethora of publications to choose from, but in a day of limited media outlets, Carmack's words were powerful. In 1931, Edward Carmack was voted the seventh most important Tennessean to have ever lived. The list read:

1. Andrew Jackson; 2. James K. Polk; 3. John Sevier; 4. Nathan Bedford Forrest; 5. Andrew Johnson; 6. Sam Houston; and 7. Edward Carmack.

Even those that disagreed with his political views respected Carmack. This made his scathing editorials extremely damaging to Patterson's political standing within the city.

It was not long before the paper started to receive hate mail and death threats in response to his editorials. This seemed to only fuel Carmack's crusade against Governor Patterson and what he stood for.

A man named Colonel Duncan Cooper was a known friend and associate of Governor Patterson, and had also been criticized by Carmack in his many editorials. One evening, Colonel Cooper and his son Robin followed Carmack on the streets of Nashville. When it seemed no one would notice, they jumped Carmack from behind and shoved him into an alley. Robin grabbed Carmack's shirt at the neck and slammed him against the brick wall. Carmack's hands clutched Robin's wrist as he tried to pry himself free with no success. He could barely breathe. Through gasps for air, he recognized one of the men as Colonel Cooper. The Colonel was less than a foot away, and Carmack could feel a revolver pressed into his ribs. Cooper's breath was hot on his face as he hissed his threats, "You're not going to write about us anymore. It's over, or you're dead. Shot in the face. Do you understand me?"

Colonel Cooper went on raving like this for a few more moments. Carmack could only shut his eyes, waiting for the gun to blast a hole in his stomach. Finally, a shot came, not from the gun, but from Robin's fist. The young man's punch sent Carmack into a wheezing fit as he slumped to the pavement holding his midsection. When he was able to catch his breath, he looked up and they were gone.

Carmack was at a crossroads. He knew the risk if he continued writing his editorials could be fatal, but could not succumb to the threats made against him. Instead of buckling under the pressure to walk away from the political fight, he purchased a gun, which he carried everywhere, and continued his quest. His editorials only raised the heat on Patterson and his affiliates.

On November 9, 1908 Carmack's editorial entitled "The Great Diplomat of the Political Zweibund" was included in that morning's edition of the *Nashville Tennessean*. The article was a comical satire of Colonel Cooper's politically corrupt connections. How furious was Colonel Cooper that morning? Upon reading the article at his kitchen table, did he smash his coffee cup against the wall in his rage? It seems possible. He was certainly angry enough about being publicly ridiculed to plot Carmack's murder.

That afternoon, at just after 4 p.m., Edward Carmack left the *Nashville Tennessean* office at 8th Avenue and Church Street for the last time. He made his way toward a drugstore across the street, and he left the store with his newly purchased soda and cigar. He walked in the direction of Union Street and ran into a couple of ladies that he knew. They stopped and talked about nothing in particular, and after a few minutes Carmack and the ladies exchanged goodbyes.

Edward Carmack started toward his apartment, which was just a street away from where he was standing on Seventh Avenue and Union Street. One of the ladies he had just been talking to screamed; he spun around to see the ambush he had entered. Colonel Duncan Cooper and Robin Cooper were both marching toward him with colt revolvers drawn. They were just a feet away when the first shot rang out drowning out the shrill screams of the two ladies. Two more shots followed ripping into his chest, and unbelievably to him his shirt was soon soaked in blood.

The two killers watched their helpless victim stumble and fall into the street. As they watched Carmack pull his hand from inside his coat, they never expected the man to reveal a gun. He fell to the ground firing off a shot in a final, desperate act of defiance. The bullet injured Robin's arm, but did not kill him. The two men walked away, leaving the two hysterical women on the street. They would later share their stories with police and reporters. Edward Carmack was dead at the age of 50.

The newspapers the next morning proclaimed him to have been a champion of free speech. One headline read: "SENATOR CARMACK IS SHOT DOWN IN COLD BLOOD – EDITOR OF *TENNESSEAN* WAYLAID AND SHOT ON THE WAY TO HIS ROOM." A line in the article read, "Because he dared to oppose the might of the saloons in Tennessee, Edward Ward Carmack lies cold in death and three gaping wounds cry out for vengeance on his murderers, Colonel Duncan B. Cooper and his son, Robin Cooper."

The day after Carmack's death, most of the businesses in Nashville were closed to mourn and honor the death of their beloved citizen. All of the government and public buildings were draped in crepe and flags were at half-mast to honor his death.

Trials followed, and both Cooper men were convicted of murder. The sentence was twenty years for each man. The story should have ended there with both men being brought to justice for their crimes, but that was not the case. Robin's conviction was overturned on a technicality, and he was mysteriously never retried. His father's conviction was upheld, but he was later pardoned by the only person with the authority to do so: Governor Malcolm Patterson.

The release of Colonel Cooper by Patterson is still viewed as one of the most egregious instances of corruption in

Tennessee's history. Historians usually refer to the entire case as the Carmack Affair.

Colonel Cooper died in bed at his home in 1922. Robin was murdered in 1918. The identity of Robin's killer or killers is a mystery to this day. There has often been speculation that Robin's murder was an act of retribution for Edward Carmack's death.

Today, a statue of Edward Carmack stands boldly in front of the State Capitol building a block away from his murder. The positioning of the monument is such that it appears that he is looking across the plaza directly at the corner where he was assassinated.

The combination of his tragic death with the lack of justice brought down on his killers has led to wide speculation about Carmack's ghost. The predominant way that this haunting seems to manifest itself is on the corner of 7th Avenue and Union Street, the site of Carmack's death. Numerous state employees and visitors have reported being near the corner and hearing three shots ring out, followed shortly by a fourth. Police are often called only to discover the area desolate.

Skeptics of ghost stories will mention that it's not uncommon to hear gunshots in urban areas, but this particular side of town is mostly government buildings and monuments, where very little crime (other than the white collar variety) is known to occur. Other theories have suggested that perhaps these are simply the backfires from older vehicles, or maybe these are gunshots from further away, and that the echoes have bounced through the plentiful skyscrapers and concrete of the downtown area.

Questions about Carmack's ghost and even his death go unanswered. Did Patterson order the killing or have knowledge himself? Is Carmack's murder still being repeated over and over again, almost begging the living not to forget? These questions linger, and Carmack's statue stands looking on, waiting for answers that may never come.

# 11

# The Haunted Tavern

econd Avetnue in downtown Nashville is one of the most historic parts of the city. Many of the city's earliest buildings have persevered in this area that's located next to the Cumberland River. It was known as Market Street when most of these stores were constructed. The 2nd Avenue stores closest to the river are enormous in depth. The reason for this is the proximity to the riverfront. In the olden days, ships would unload their goods on the docks, which then could be delivered directly into the backsides of the stores. The grains, wood, or clothing would be stored in the back and sold out of the storefronts facing Market Street. The stores were both warehouse and storefront, which explains the vastness of the buildings today.

At present time, the area is full of nightlife. Restaurants, showcases, and dance clubs abound in the most vibrant part of downtown. One such location is a bar called Buffalo Billiards. The club has been a mainstay of the city, outlasting many of the other "fly by night" bars in the area. It's one of the largest buildings on the block; so much so that the bottom level is an entirely different club called Coyote Ugly.

Pool tables fill the cavernous, brick building with its Wild West theme. A favorite of locals and tourists alike, it's also said to be patronized by one of the area's best-known specters. Some of the bartenders and retailers in the area have called him the "Confederate Ghost," though it's believed that he is not really a Confederate at all. However his clothing has been mistaken as such.

The spirit is said to have been one of the early warehouse workers there when the building stored and sold iron and

Buffalo Billiard's is located on 2ⁿᵈ Avenue, which was once known as Market Street.

metal goods. One day, a tall stack of crates and boxes fell over, crushing the man to death. Other than that, little is known about him ... except for the accounts of his appearances post mortem.

When the current nightclub's owner first opened for business, it wasn't long before this spirit made its presence known. The owner, a barrel-chested man who was always dressed in fashionable, well-pressed shirts and carefully styled hair, was passing through one of the rooms closest to the side facing the river. The tall windows allowed the morning sun into the otherwise dark room. The sun's rays gave the room a yellow glow, illuminating the dust particles in the air. Out of the corner of his eye, he saw a man standing in the corner near the windows. He turned to get a better look, but the man was gone.

A reasonable man, he assumed at the time that his mind had a played a trick on him, and that the "man" had merely been a shadow formed by the sun. Future sightings later proved this theory to be incorrect.

He has claimed to have seen this man fifteen to twenty times over the years. Usually the man would emerge next to the same windows, wearing a cap, gloves, dark boots, and gray worker's coveralls (the clothing being the reason that so many have mistaken him for a Rebel soldier). His appearance is always described as if he's partly invisible, like a fading photograph.

The owner said that whenever the man would appear, he'd always turn quickly, trying to get a better look at him. He learned, though, that instead of looking directly at the image, if he kept his gaze in the original direction, the image would last longer. Sometimes he would stay twenty or more seconds before disappearing completely.

Others have confirmed the owner's sightings. The downtown bartenders and servers are an incestuous bunch, often bouncing around from one bar to the next. They become pretty familiar with everyone on 2$^{nd}$ Avenue and have spread their stories around. Not only have many of them seen the man in the same area, he has also frequently been seen downstairs in the liquor room. One bartender entered the room to restock his bar for the next day ... and sensed someone else was there. It was a dank, dungeon-like room lit by a single, low wattage bulb hanging in the center and the bartender realized someone or something was behind him. At first he thought maybe it was a large rat, which would have been frightening enough. He turned slowly so as not to show fear—and realized that there was *ANOTHER* man in the room with him.

The bartender was frozen solid with his hands full of whiskey bottles. The stranger was barely discernable in the shadows. He seemed to be looking at him, and the bartender waited with anticipation of an attack. But the man seemed to step back, disappearing into the darkness behind him. After a second, the bartender was moving again. In a panic, he shoved the bottles back on their shelves and fetched a lighter out of his pocket with a fumbling grasp. His hands trembled as he flicked the lighter, making small sparks with each failed attempt. Once he caught a flame, he cupped the lighter with his palm and walked toward the dark. He was alone. He never talked about this to anyone...until he overheard some of his co-workers telling similar stories.

Management has also reported trouble with the security cameras. In the office, there are about a dozen video monitors. Being motion sensitive, the video screens only pop on if someone enters the camera's field of vision in the room. On a number of occasions, a nighttime manager has been sitting in the office finishing up paperwork, when one of the video screens has turned on. Alone in the building, the manager watches with interest as one screen after another hums to life in a pattern that would indicate that someone was passing through the building—even though no one is visible on the monitor.

They contacted the security company responsible for the system, and after the technicians examined the equipment, they declared everything to be in working order. Despite the assurances of the security company, the problem has persisted. The general manager even went through the building with a ladder and a broom, sweeping in front of the cameras in case cobwebs or spiders were causing the problem. Still, the cameras continued to record seemingly empty rooms.

More than the video cameras or even the visual confirmations, the most memorable experience the owner noted happened when he was alone in the upstairs office. He was at his desk in the middle of the afternoon while half a dozen men were nursing beers downstairs. The owner sat huddled over his desk, checking inventory sheets with a pen in his hand. Like most nightclub offices in the country, the room was full of file cabinets, an assortment of novelty cups, and stacks of paperwork in every conceivable space.

He was deeply engrossed in the numbers before him when, from behind, he could feel that something was falling. He didn't hear a creak or see anything, but could feel the movement in the room. Instinctively, he closed his eyes and braced for the stack of files that was inevitably falling behind him.

There was a tremendous crash, but the owner was unhurt. He opened his eyes, prepared to clean up the mess. Everything was fine. The papers hadn't moved an inch. Knowing that the noise had not been his imagination, he thought that maybe a bartender had accidentally dropped a case of liquor or rack of glasses downstairs. He hustled down the steps and asked the bartender, "Is everything okay?" He surveyed the room, looking for broken glass.

"Yeah, why?" the tattooed bartender answered, stepping from the regulars.

"There was a crash, you had to have heard that." He looked out the large front window, wondering if maybe it had been a car crash.

"No, I didn't hear anything," he said in a way that made it clear to the owner that he wasn't lying. It started to dawn on the owner that maybe this was again the ghost, perhaps reliving the crash of crates that had taken his life.

One of the smiling regulars chimed in, "I think somebody's been drinking on the job." All of his cronies at the bar laughed at their buddy, and the owner's face grew red as he walked away. He thought to himself that spirits had been the problem, all right. Just not the kind of spirits they thought.

# 12

# Living in the Past

On the south side of Nashville, many of the city's finest and most historic homes can be found. The rolling hills in the area made it an ideal site for many of Nashville's wealthiest citizens to build houses. Near Brown's Creek and Franklin Pike on what is known as Breeze Hill, one of these many exquisite homes once stood. A man named Joseph Vaulx built the mansion in the early 1800s. A Revolutionary war veteran, he had moved his family from the Carolinas to settle in Nashville.

After years of work, the home was completed in 1832. It was worth the wait. It was considered by his contemporaries to be one of the most immaculate and spectacular plantation homes in the area. The Vaulx family amassed a great deal of wealth, and Joseph's children prospered in the home. As with many plantations in the area, the Civil War changed everything. The location made it a valuable commodity for both sides of the war. It was located near a major road, making its elevated site a strategically enviable possession.

The Vaulx family watched helplessly as their crops and cattle were poached by occupying Union forces. The Confederates didn't do them any favors either. Although they would pay the family with Confederate currency for their goods, the outcome of the war made the paper money virtually worthless.

The Battle of Nashville in 1864 proved to be the last major conflict in the western theatre of the war. It was pivotal and bloody. Breeze Hill was located on the Confederate lines. The Rebels occupied the large estate, using it as both a headquarters and hospital. Maimed Confederates were dragged up the hill and given aid in the home. The lucky ones received crude amputations to save them from deadly infections and their screams could be heard rolling down the hillside from the Vaulx mansion. The unlucky would die on the home's hardwood floors, their lifeless eyes looking blankly at the ceiling above.

In the midst of the chaos, the makeshift headquarters saw a rare female visitor. A woman rode near the hill with her leg dangling awkwardly on her steed. Barely hanging on to the reigns of her horse, the Rebels who approached her on horseback thought she might slide off any second. She told them she had fallen off her horse, injuring herself.

The soldiers escorted her back to the home on Breeze Hill so that she could rest and heal her twisted leg. That night, Confederate officers were in a large parlor. With maps sprawled out on tables that had been gathered from all over the house, the men discussed strategies. The officers were all haggard looking, some with bandages and bloodstained uniforms. Exhausted from days of battle, they quarreled and debated their next moves. The fate of the Confederate army was upon them, and they knew the next few days' moves would either spare them more time or give the Union army victory.

Suddenly, a scream screeched out from the adjoining room. It was a woman's voice. Several of the officers rushed into the hall to find the body of the lady visitor lying on the ground at the base of the steep and winding staircase.

It was later determined that the woman was a Union spy. They believed that she was sent by the Union with the thought that the "Southern gentlemen" would take in their damsel in distress and they were right. It was a tactic not uncommonly employed throughout the war. They later theorized that she must have been listening from the top of the stairs, not far from the room the soldiers had given her. Perhaps she had been unable to hear their strategies and by leaning further out over the railing had lost her balance. She had hit the staircase a few times in her long drop to the bottom and was probably dead before she even hit the floor.

After the war, the Vaulx family struggled to piece their lives back together. They lived in Nashville, but the mansion was often empty. The war had taken its toll on the Breeze Hill home, and with the days of plantation life now firmly planted in the past, care for the home's condition was of little importance.

The last of the Vaulx line died at the home in 1908. The home was vacant for years. Broken shudders dangled, barely hanging onto the walls; the yard was full of weeds and fallen trees; areas of the fence were broken or missing completely. Without light, the silhouette of the massive, dilapidated home on Breeze Hill captured the dark imaginations of the children that lived in the surrounding neighborhoods. Ghost stories were rampant. Children dared each other to run up to the front door, knock, and then run back—like a scene out of *To Kill a Mockingbird*.

In the 1920s, a man named Morris Wilson purchased the house and restored it. Famous for its parties, it was once again full of life. After his death, his daughter Elizabeth and her husband, William Scribner, moved into the home. It wasn't long before the home's past made itself known to its new occupants.

Early one morning, Mr. Scribner was shaving at the bathroom sink. In the steamy mirror, he could see his wife enter. He began talking about a variety of different topics. The conversation was largely one-sided, as his wife answered only in brief, single word answers. As he carefully guided his straight edge razor across his face, William continued to talk about travel plans and trouble at work to his wife, who was sitting on a small chair behind him; he never turned to see the woman behind him.

Several minutes later, near the end of his shave, the door opened again, and in the mirror, William could see another woman there. He turned to find his wife, who was entering with an armful of fresh and folded towels.

William dropped his razor in the sink and spun around to the chair. It was empty. His jaw hung open comically.

Elizabeth was heading toward the linen closet paying no interest to her husband's surprise. "I didn't know you were the kind to talk to yourself."

"I'm not. I was talking to you," he said trying to determine how his wife had been in two places at once.

"To me? You weren't talking to me. You must be losing your mind, William," she said.

"I must," he was shaking his head in disbelief. "Elizabeth, are you serious? You really weren't here, just minutes ago, talking to me?"

"No. I walked in and you were talking about a vacation or something," Elizabeth said, now curious. She set the towels down.

"Then who was that who came in and sat down behind me fifteen minutes ago?" William breezed past his wife glancing quickly inside the small linen closet. It was empty.

His face was stern and still flecked with bits of shaving cream. Again he brushed past his wife, nearly knocking her over, as he made his way into the hallway. He looked up and down the halls and then systematically checked each bedroom. He looked under beds, in closets, and behind furniture with his bride following from behind.

"William, you're scaring me," she said, secretly wondering about her husband's state of mind.

"Someone is here. I talked to her. She's here somewhere."

He continued his search, but the home was empty and the front door was locked. William later surmised that Elizabeth had played a joke on him even though she swore she hadn't.

Weeks later, the Scribners had a friend from out of town visit for the weekend, and on one night, they were awakened by a commotion upstairs.

William ran up the staircase and found their guest coming out of his room in a rush. His friend's hair was tussled, and he struggled to adjust his eyes to the hallway.

"Was that you?" he asked William accusingly.

"What's wrong? I heard a noise, like the roof caved in."

"I fell out of bed or more like I jumped out." He looked down the hall. "Who was that in my bed?"

He looked at William, who was stunned and unsure what to say, "In your bed?"

"I was asleep, I rolled over and felt someone, a woman, I thought, right there beside me. I must have jumped ten feet in the air."

William looked in the guest room door to see the disheveled bedspread and an overturned lamp and vase by the bed. He was reminded of his conversation with a woman who was (or wasn't) sitting behind him in the washroom weeks before.

After a few seconds, his friend asked, "Where's your wife?"

"My wife?" he answered, and then it dawned on him what his guest was implying. "My wife was in bed with me," he said with conviction.

"You're sure?"

"I'm certain," he said unhappy with this line of questioning. "Clearly you had too much wine tonight. Maybe you should sleep it off."

There was a chill in the air between them, but his guest went back to bed still confused about his experience. William made his way back to the bedroom wondering if his friend really was a little drunk from dinner, or if maybe their two experiences were some how related. Elizabeth was still awake when he returned to their bedroom. He told her what had happened. Elizabeth nodded as he talked, but said nothing herself. Her brow was furrowed in a way that her husband knew meant that she too was starting to have the same thoughts.

Their deepest fears were realized weeks later. One Sunday morning, Elizabeth and William were sitting, in leather chairs, across from each other reading newspapers and talking with steaming cups of tea nearby each of them. It was Elizabeth's favorite time of the week with her husband, enjoying the conversation and pattering rain outside the window. The room had a bluish gray tint due to the weather outside. William was talking about an article that he had read about a man named Adolf Hitler and how the editor speculated that soon the United States might have to engage him in war. Elizabeth thought this nonsense; that the country would not soon again enter into war in Europe after so recently losing thousands of lives in the Great War.

As they were talking, Elizabeth turned and carefully picked up her teacup and saucer, so as not to spill any of the hot liquid on her legs. As she brought the cup to her lips, over the rim she saw someone standing in the corner. William, who was not facing the direction of the woman, watched as his wife dropped her cup and saucer. The cup cracked on the wooden floors like an egg, but the saucer first landed on her knee and then the top of her foot before reaching the ground undamaged. Elizabeth seemed to make no effort to stop the fall. Her bottom lip was quivering in a way William had never seen. The saucer was spinning like a top loudly for what seemed like forever before finally petering out and coming to rest inches from her chair leg.

William followed Elizabeth's eyes to the bookshelf behind him. In the corner, a woman with dark hair and old-fashioned clothing was standing there, watching them. *It's her,* William thought, as the stranger started walking toward them. Elizabeth let out her breath, creating a moaning sound. William jumped to his feet. "What are you doing here?" he demanded.

She gave no answer, but only walked toward his desk. "Answer me," he said, less confident. There seemed to be something wrong with her skin color. It was like she was sick.

Just before she reached the desk, William remembered a revolver that he kept there, and for a split second thought she meant to retrieve it. "Stop or…" but he did not finish the thought. The intruder did not kneel down for the gun hidden in one of its drawers, but kept walking straight *through* the desk.

William was speechless, struggling to comprehend what he was seeing. Elizabeth was feeling the same. The woman's bottom half disappeared as she walked into the oak desk. Her upper torso remained moving forward it seemed without any pain to her. When her top half reached the end of the desk, her gray colored dress, legs, and feet all reappeared. Elizabeth had pulled her feet off the ground as if a mouse had scampered into the room. William started to step forward and thought better of it. Instead he watched as the woman neared with his eyes blinking rapidly.

The woman stopped walking. William dared a quick look at his wife. She had an expression on her face that he had not seen since the day she had learned of her father's death. He turned his attention back to the impossible woman, who was standing in the middle of his study. He wondered if she would next fly into the air.

She looked at him, or past him, with a look on her face as if she were about to ask a question. Her mouth was slightly open, and her head tilted a bit to one side. William could see his desk behind her. He blinked thinking this was the beginning of him passing out, but realized the woman was disappearing. It made him think of looking at his own reflection in a pond, being able to see yourself but also the pebbles beneath the water's surface.

She was gone. The woman hadn't walked out the door or crawled out a window. She had simply disappeared, like a carnival magician. Except here, no one was applauding.

The following months were unbearable for them. Every time a floorboard creaked or someone knocked unexpectedly at the door, their hearts would feel like they had turned into lead. An out of place chair or partially opened door was enough to make them feel out of their minds. Other strange things occurred (none as strange as that Sunday afternoon) and they decided they couldn't live there anymore. They soon moved out, but had a caretaker move in to look after the expensive home.

Unaware of the Scribners' encounters, the caretaker later told the couple of one of her own unexplained episodes. One cold, January morning, she awoke in her bed. She was drenched in sweat. The woman pulled the quilts off of her and saw a roaring fire in the fireplace.

The caretaker told them this and looked at them, waiting. The Scribners did not catch the significance, and they looked questioningly at each other, the way married couples do. The caretaker took an exasperated breath, like a frustrated teacher having to reveal the answer to the simplest of problems, "I didn't go to bed with quilts. They had all been in the closet, and I didn't start a fire."

She watched as the Scribners' faces dawned with understanding. If the caretaker had been hoping for some kind of explanation from them, she was disappointed. They told her she must have been sleepwalking, or simply forgotten, perhaps overly tired. But they knew better.

Elizabeth's love for the home her father had put so much work and care into restoring proved to be stronger than her fear of its otherworldly inhabitant. They moved back into the home and learned to live with the ghost there. Over the years, while having dinner, they would stop talking briefly as they could hear someone walking up the stairs in the next room. They would resume their conversation often without a word about the noise they had heard.

It's amazing what the human mind can accomplish. Even the most extraordinary occurrences can become ordinary with time and experience. This proved to be the case for the Scribners, who learned to drown out the ghost like someone accustomed to living next door to a train station, no longer cognizant of the noise. The house servants were another matter entirely. The employees rotated through the house like children on a carousel.

The Scribners left the home for a final time in 1961. They still owned the mansion and employed another caretaker to look after the estate. This new caretaker proved to be incompetent and rarely even visited the home, pocketing his salary over the next decade. Thieves stripped the house of its valuable furniture, sculptures, and paintings; vandals left graffiti and broken windows; and squatters moved in at one point and burned the remaining furniture in the middle of the living room.

The home was in deplorable condition, more than it had been after 1908. Elizabeth Scribner asked a man named John Bell (not to be confused with John Bell of Adams, Tennessee and the famous Bell Witch) if he would be interested in restoring the mansion. She was at an age and place in life where she could no longer care for her once lovely manor and take on the job of rebuilding it. Bell, who had an appreciation for historic homes, was interested but declined. He felt the task was too monumental.

In 1973, John Bell's friends, Wayne Bottoms and Robert Bolanger, agreed to help him restore the home. Enthused with his friends' willingness to help him, he contacted Elizabeth. She was thrilled to have him as the new caretaker and contractor. They used all of their connections and relatives to help them with their endeavor.

Being young men, they were excited about the task. John moved into the home, and when his friends' had free time, they would work on the house. The job was even more difficult than they had anticipated. Rotten wood, cracked tiles, mildew, and leaks filled every inch of the home. This would have been complicated enough—even without the unexpected and more frightening obstacles.

Like everyone else that had ever lived or worked in the home, the home's restless spirit soon made its presence known to the three men. Creaks, bangs, and other odd sounds were not unusual, but were immediately dismissed as typical of an aging home.

One evening, the three were on hands and knees laying new tile in one of the downstairs bathrooms. From the main hall, where the grand staircase was, came a tremendous crash. The men looked at each other in surprise as they could hear *SOMETHING* topple down the stairs. They ran out of the bathroom together, expecting to find a broken section of banister or fallen chunk of rotten ceiling at the bottom.

In the center of the room, a woman in a gray dress was laying sprawled on the floor. Her head was twisted awkwardly at the neck and a small pool of blood formed near her mouth. The men each offered a few curse words at the gruesome sight, but Bell rushed up to the obviously injured woman. He stood over her unsure what to do. Should he roll her over? Her neck looked broken, and he feared injuring her further.

He turned to the other two, "Go call 911."

Neither of the men moved at first, and then Robert turned and dashed off, presumably to find a phone. Wayne, who had never taken his eyes off the dead woman, blinked hard a couple of times and said almost stoically, "John, she's gone."

Thinking he meant 'gone' as in dead, he looked down at the floor and realized he meant 'gone' as in '*gone*.'

This occurred several times over the next few months. Sometimes the woman would be at the base of the stairs. Once in a while, they would be hammering away and would look up across the room to see their phantom lady standing there. They came to call her the Gray Lady, and eventually asked Elizabeth Scribner about her.

She told John all about the woman and how she had been haunting the home for decades. John listened in fascination as she told the story of the Union spy who had fallen to her death at the pinnacle of the Battle of Nashville. She said she knew for certain that this lady was haunting the home, but she believed there were others....

John learned this to be not only true, but also an understatement.

John often had friends stay at the home; they were curious about his work and the home itself. One October, John greeted a friend at the door and then left him there to answer the phone. His friend looked out the window in the foyer to admire the view from Breeze Hill. He could see past the drive to the house, a breath-taking view of miles of red, golden, and orange trees of autumn. The rooftops of little houses poked up through the treetops. From this height, he could see dozens of roads cutting paths through the woods. Even further, he could see the skyline of the downtown office buildings.

Without any transition, the homes and roads disappeared out of view, apparently covered by the green leaves (green?) of the trees below. The skyscrapers were gone. Where enormous maples and oak trees had stood there was little more than slender saplings. The telephone poles, cars, electrical towers, airplanes, water towers, and even the faint sound of traffic in the distance were all gone. All of the signs of fall were suddenly gone, replaced by the vibrant greens of a summer's day. The shock was dizzying. He felt his knees buckle, but did not fall.

From his left hand view through the window, he noticed movement. A horse and carriage made its way up the steep and winding path. A man and woman emerged from around the house dressed in Civil War era type of clothing. The man and woman were smiling at the arriving carriage.

The man looked around the foyer. While the outside had changed, the inside had not. Scraps of wood, worktables, and sawdust filled the room indicating the ongoing work of a home in repair.

"John, come here," he called turning back to the window, "John?"

John didn't answer, apparently still on the phone down the hall. More carriages pulled up, one after another, unloading their passengers. Each couple was dressed more elaborately than the last. Women in blue, pink, lavender, and yellow Southern belle gowns were escorted from the carriages by their escorts, and each woman raised her parasol apparently to protect herself from the sun's rays.

The houseguest felt a little like Dorothy in the *Wizard of Oz,* as he watched this incredible train of carriages continue to parade up to the house. He considered running out the front door, but feared that he might lose this remarkable...well, what was it exactly? Ghosts from the past? A hallucination? Had he traveled through time? He waited, in awe of the sight.

Several minutes went by and then... it was *gone.* The once green grass was covered in piles of red and yellow leaves. The homes and buildings at the bottom of the hillside reappeared, protruding through the landscape with jarring surprise. It was all gone.

The guest let out a long breath that he hadn't realized he was holding; he found himself saddened a little by the loss of the image. The more modern world suddenly seemed so dirty and gray, and he was surprised by his newfound melancholy. John returned and could see that something was wrong with his friend. John looked toward the stairway and wondered if his guest had witnessed a woman tumbling and falling down three flights of stairs before finally snapping her neck at the bottom. If so, he might have a lot to explain.

They talked for some time about the men and women the friend had seen moments before, stepping out of the past, graceful and carefree. He expressed how pleasant and soothing the whole thing was. John also shared his stories about the Gray Lady and her recurring death on the stairs.

John wasn't sure what to make of his friend's 'time travel.' It seemed very different from his previous encounters. Later that winter, John was cleaning the floors in one of the living areas, scrubbing at a particular dark and resilient stain on the floor. He stroked at the sticky, black stain faster and faster, frustrated with the effort. Sweat dripped from his nose, landing on the boards below in little splotches. John stopped briefly to regain his strength and started up again.

The stain came right out in a single wipe. It was amazing, and John leaned back a little to see. In fact, the floor looked immaculate. He could almost smell the wood in the air—**AND** something else. Smoke filled his nose, and he saw a man in a white shirt and long sideburns standing at the window. He held a pipe in one hand, and with the other he was pulling slightly at the drapes – wait, there hadn't been drapes there before! – to peek outside. The sun from outside the window illuminated his face slightly. How was this possible? It was nearly ten at night!

Then suddenly, he was gone. The smoke, daylight, and drapes vanished, and the room returned to normal, even the smudge on the floor was back. It had only lasted a few seconds, but John was convinced this was not his imagination. This went on for months. John and his partners frequently took these little jumps into the past; the images always gave them the impression of being in the mid 1800s.

In ways he couldn't understand, John came to believe that somehow the ghosts in the home were affecting the passage of time itself. He and his friends constantly found themselves resetting clocks and watches. They would lose track of time when in the home and often had trouble remembering which day of the week it was.

This time slippage, or whatever it was, impacted them in other ways. John would leave one room with a large painting of a mountain scene and a babbling brook hanging over the mantle, only to discover the same painting was miraculously hanging in the new room he had just entered. On occasion, they would get lost in the house, almost as if the rooms had 'shifted.' Their time at the Breeze Hill mansion was very disorienting.

It would have been bearable, even with the Gray Lady and the glimpses into the past, but there was something else, something **MALEVOLENT** in the home as well. They would notice shadows sliding across the walls, and unlike the almost enchanting scenes from a romantic southern landscape, these dark shapes were unnerving. They seemed to be watching them and waiting. This was something they didn't articulate to each other, but rather something they felt just below their conscious minds.

That spring, on a particularly cool afternoon, Wayne had finished painting one of the bedrooms. With coveralls specked in white and brown paint, he made his way to the stairs, absently picking at the dried paint on his nails. As he neared the top of the staircase, he heard – or maybe he *felt* – someone approaching from behind him. Before he could turn to look, he felt someone or something slam into his back with force. He fell toward the balcony railing unable to stop. His waist crashed into the rail, and his momentum flipped him head over heels. The impact knocked the wind out of his lungs.

He flipped over the banister with arms and legs flailing like a mad gymnast, but somehow he managed to grab the banister with his right arm. His arm was hooked through the slender beam at the elbow. Distantly, he was aware of his throbbing side, which he would later learn was a busted rib. His heart pounded and his vision blurred, but he looked down to see the thirty-foot drop to the floor below. He watched as some loose coins that had apparently flown out of his pockets during his somersault fall fly toward the ground below. Upon impact with the hardwoods below, the pennies and quarters made a rapid-fire sound, like a machine gun firing off, and bounced and rolled away in sporadic directions.

Wayne thought briefly of the Gray Lady. He felt his elbow slip, and he struggled to hold on. His feet dangled below, and Wayne tried to figure out how he could pull himself back up. He looked through the rails, hoping for something to grab, but saw nothing – had he seen a shadow, fading back into the walls? – that could help him. He looked back down at his feet dangling below. He wasn't sure just how long he could stay this way. Wayne tried to call out for help, but his call came out as a wheeze. He was still trying to catch his breath.

John came out of a hallway downstairs wiping his hands with a towel with an air of casualness that made Wayne start to feel panic and a little displaced anger at his friend for not realizing the immediate danger. It was clear to Wayne that John had heard his near fall, but had assumed it to be another of the Gray Lady's hauntings.

"John," he tried to call out, but it was barely a whisper, and Wayne knew he couldn't hear him from so far away.

John continued to dry his hands with his stupid towel. As he walked through the room beneath Wayne, John continued to survey the floor for any appearances of the dead lady. With the calm of a man looking at his lawn to determine if it needs watering, he strolled around in mindless circles. John stopped and knelt down, and reached for one of Wayne's quarters on the ground.

"John," Wayne managed a little louder, but it was still not enough. The feelings of helplessness and doom started to take over his mind. He slipped a bit more, and readjusted. From this height, Wayne would have to shout for John to hear him. John stood and started to walk away. The horror was really starting to set in. He was going to fall and die, just like that woman. John would come back to find him lying there with bug eyes and a dozen broken bones. He felt the muscles in his arm begin to ache and throb. John was halfway to the door, and Wayne knew his situation would be a million times worse if he walked out of the room. The chances of him hearing him then would be…

The way out of this appeared to him clearly in his mind and he moved to action. He kicked at his boot with his foot. Over and over he pushed at the top of his heavy work boot, trying to pry it free. He dangled and swayed overhead as he did so. The laces were tight, and he struggled between trying to wedge the boot off and not losing his grip on the banister. Finally the boot started to move, and once it loosened, it slid right past his ankle and foot with ease.

The boot almost seemed to hiss as it cut through the air on its long collision course with the hardwood floors below. The boot smacked the floorboards with a thud, and John Bell turned around.

He stood there for what seemed to Wayne like hours. *Look up already. Come on buddy. I'm right here.*

Mercifully John gazed up. His jaw fell open, and Wayne could see the emotions of confusion, surprise, shock, and fear spread across his face in seconds. John charged up the stairs.

"Wayne, hold on, I'm coming!" he called out as he leaped up the steps in twos and threes. Knowing that John was on his way, he closed his eyes and concentrated on his one mission. *Don't let go. Don't let go.* He repeated the mantra over and over trying to focus on this singular task.

He could feel hands slide under his arms pulling him up. There was a second when John felt his weight shift, and he thought they were both going to go toppling over the edge together. John re-anchored his legs and pulled harder. In an instant, Wayne was over the rail and they tumbled in a heap on top of each other.

Wayne found his head on John's chest, and exhausted and out of breath, they stayed that way for a moment. And then, as often happens when people barely escape death, they started laughing. They laughed for a while, the sound echoing through the old halls.

After this incident, John Bell decided that he had had enough of these ghosts. Knocking sounds and visions were one thing, but these darker forces convinced him that the home was unsafe. He called upon the services of a well-respected Nashvillian named Mildred Cowan. A religious and educated woman, she had seen ghosts, and through a variety of prayers and rituals, had extinguished a ghost from her home. Others learned of her abilities and it wasn't long before she was called on to do so for others. Families, embarrassed by what others might think of them, would ask her in confidence to come to their homes in hopes of ridding them of any unwanted spirits.

Mildred came to the mansion on Breeze Hill, happy to help John with his problem. She chanted, read Biblical passages, prayed, and talked to the home's spirits. This lasted for hours, and John was both hopeful and skeptical of her abilities. The next few days seemed to reveal that Mildred's efforts were futile. He could 'feel' the ghosts still lurking in the home and believed that he may have to leave the home he had come to love as much as Elizabeth did.

Not quite a week after Mildred had attempted to cleanse the home of spirits, John was asleep in his room. He rolled over in bed and could see a faint light across the bedroom floor. He sat up in bed rubbing his eyes. The bedroom door was closed, but in the narrow space between the floor and the base of the door, he could see a yellow light coming through. Its glow spread across the floor, fading in brightness as it approached his bed. Behind the door, the light seemed to move like someone was pacing there.

Alone in the house, John wondered what business the ghosts were up to now. He slid out of bed and followed the light to the door. The wood creaked under his feet. He grabbed the brass knob and turned. Golden light filled the bedroom, and John squinted at its brightness. He staggered forward as his eyes adjusted from the darkness. He slept on the second floor, and made his way toward the hall where the staircase was located.

More than the carriages, southern belles and gentlemen, dark shadows, the dead gray woman, and even the near death encounter with Wayne, the center of the vast room held the most amazing sight he had seen in his years there. A pillar of light stood in the middle of the room, surrounded by the winding, wooden staircase. It reached from the floor to the ceiling, and John's mind had a hard time comprehending it. It seemed alive and spiraled upward. His ears were buzzing with a distant hum, and John was mesmerized by the light. He thought he had seen it all, but again was proven wrong.

He watched the yellow light twist slowly on its axis, wondering what he should do. It occurred to him that he may not be safe there, but there was no way he could leave this room. He was very much like the moth to a flame.

The spiraling light tower seemed to not be touching the ceiling as it had before. John started to feel his eyes were adjusting to the glow, but soon realized that it was not him. The column of light was fading.

In seconds the tower was half its previous height, and the darkness was starting to creep back in. Not sure why he was doing it, he started moving down the stairs never taking his eyes off of the shrinking light. Soon it was little more than a half-foot tall and lit the small space of floor with the power of a night-light. It seemed to flicker, almost getting brighter for a second, and then disappeared. John was left standing on the stairs in the complete darkness.

The following months proved that Mildred had been successful. The haunting had ceased. There had not been anymore dead women found on the floors. The Southern belles of the past seemed content to stay in their own place in history. Clocks kept time. Objects stayed put. Shadows were shadows. And... the home was *DYING*.

It seemed that at every turn, the home provided a new challenge. The roof was springing more leaks than ever before. He discovered termites in many areas of the home that had seemed fine previously. Wood was rotting, plumbing sprung leaks, paint peeled, and areas of the walls and the ceiling would fall in chunks. The house was coming apart at a rate that John couldn't keep up with. He felt like he was fighting a forest fire with a water glass.

The financial burden started to outweigh the love for the old mansion, and the Scribner family decided to sell it in 1983. It was bulldozed to the ground, and a neighborhood of comparatively bland three and four bedroom homes were built all around Breeze Hill.

John had mixed emotions about the home's fate. He felt relieved, but also a little guilty. Was it possible to kill a home? It seemed silly to think this way. A home, even a mansion, is simply wood, windows, and nails. It's not a living thing. John tried to convince himself of this, but in his heart, he knew better.

# 13

# Last Stop at Union Station

O ne of the grandest buildings in downtown Nashville is Union Station. Construction began in 1898 and it was opened to great fanfare in 1900. Highly anticipated, the opening of the train station was celebrated with fireworks and parades. The most high-ranking of Tennessee's politicians offered speeches and everyone was anxious to visit the building. The new station meant that Nashville should enjoy great prosperity as a key hub to the growing railway industry, and many felt the station was decades overdue. Revenues were expected to follow benefiting, directly or indirectly, all of the citizens.

Besides the economic impact of the structure, the aesthetics of the new train station were a marvel as well. The chief civil engineer on the project was Major Eugene Lewis. His vision was the chief influence on the structure. The enormous Richardson Romanesque building boasted a tall clock tower with the world's first digital clock. It was capped with a statue of Mercury, visible from all over Nashville. Mercury was adopted as a symbol of commerce and transportation, doubly fitting for the town known as "the Athens of the South." With a flair for the outrageous, Major Lewis had twin alligator pools installed as well. Huge slabs of limestone were carved on site, producing steep towers and palatial archways throughout the building. The main hall was breathtaking with its barrel vaulted, Tiffany-style stained glass windows, which to this day remain. In its archways, along the walls, twenty statues of angels encircled the room. Each angel held a different item of commerce in her hands that ranked as one of the top twenty in importance at the time: wheat, livestock, tobacco, books, and cotton are but a few. They are placed in order of volume one through twenty. Interestingly, the first angelic statue holds a

**Union Station was once the hub of Nashville's commerce as a train station, but is now one of the finest historic hotels in Tennessee.**

beer mug. Originally painted, today the ivory colored statues are trimmed with gold.

Its glory days saw countless young men offering tearful goodbyes during both World Wars, and sadly also saw many of them return in rows of coffins. Franklin D. Roosevelt entered through the station on his trip to Nashville. The notorious Al Capone entered the station on his way to prison. Handcuffed to a rail in his boxcar and surrounded by dozens of FBI agents, hundreds of Nashvillians ogled at the gangster from walkways above his train car.

There were also a few murders committed there. One story is that a furiously jealous man shot his girlfriend's husband in the middle of the train station. He bolted outside, but was tackled by security and captured.

As the importance of railways passed, so did the importance of Union Station. The last passenger train departed Union Station in 1978. The doors were closed and the building's future was uncertain. Union Station was close to becoming a state office building. The grandeur of the station made preserving it desirable to its citizens, but the problem was how to make this feasible.

Some creative investors and architects revealed a plan to remodel Union Station and to transform it into a hotel. The plan would spare most of the beauty and allure of the station, while modernizing it enough to make it profitable.

In 1986, the hotel opened, pleasing most of the city. Each room was unique, and the investors' gamble paid off. The boarding area with the stained glass windows overhead was transformed into the main lobby and reception desk. It was a success, and is operating as one of the downtown's most respected hotels. In fact, it's so popular that it seems one guest *refuses* to leave.

As hotel employees everywhere can attest, they are often witness to some of the most lascivious and eyebrow-raising romantic liaisons one can imagine. Frequently, hotels are host to romantic affairs that would make a soap opera writer blush. One of the hotel's ghost stories involves a couple whose story in many ways is common, but the unusual aftermath of their tale has caused it to resonate for years.

Older employees at Union Station Hotel recalled a couple that met there once every month, usually on the weekends. They would sometimes check in together, but mostly hours apart. For front desk clerks, discretion is an unspoken requirement of the job. The man never wore a wedding band, although the thin, white tan line on his left finger revealed that somewhere (his glove compartment or coat pocket, perhaps) a ring existed, and no doubt a wife. The couple frequently ordered breakfast in their room in the morning and bottles of expensive champagne at night. She would often answer the door in a terrycloth robe (day or night) with tussled hair and a pinkish glow on her cheeks. In the lobby they were always in each other's arms, kissing and giggling into each other's ear the way that only those having affairs can.

The hotel employees never batted an eye. The clerks would smile in their customer service trained fashion and slide the affectionate couple their keys with, "I hope you enjoy your stay. I will be at the desk the rest of the evening if you need anything." Who knew what lives they left at home and what stories they told their families? Watching torrid affairs like this one has caused more than one idealistic employee to become a cynic in the world of love and romance.

One weekend, the lady checked in at the desk before her lover. He didn't check in that evening, and she called the clerks a couple of times that night to see if he had left her a message. He hadn't. The next day came and went, and again, he had not checked in. As far as anyone could tell, she didn't leave the room for days. Room service was called on repeatedly. The second day, a server was called to her room, which was number 711, and he could see the change in her demeanor instantly. Always talkative and friendly, today she was curt, not even making eye contact, when he delivered her sandwich to her room. Her makeup was smudged, and her eyes were red as if she hadn't slept all night or had been crying for hours. Both were probably true.

Through the door he could see a dozen or so used tissues scattered in little balls all around the room. The drapes were closed. Less than half a bottle of vodka sat in the center of a small table. There was some broken glass of some kind in the corner, possibly from a tumbler or a picture frame. He turned back to her and realized she had seen him examining her room. He felt his face flush with embarrassment. Looking at her eyes again and her expression, he realized she was drunk. No, not drunk, hammered.

Despite his instincts, his moral code compelled him to say, "Ma'am, is everything okay?" Once again, he looked toward the broken glass and liquor before looking back at her, as if to point out the reason for his concern. He had broken the invisible wall between server and customer. She did not appreciate it.

Her face twisted, and she stumbled from one foot to the next in the way that only the highly inebriated can. "Get out. Just get out," her eyes were half open as she said this.

"I'm sorry, I didn't mean..." he started to say backing up, "It just seems..."

She pulled a few dollar bills from somewhere and threw them into the hall at his feet. "Leave me alone. Get out of my room," she slurred trying to convey her anger, but he only felt pity for her. The door closed and he could hear the deadbolt. He stood there a moment before bending to pick up the tip. He would be the last person to see her alive.

As far as anyone could tell, she didn't leave the room for dinner that evening or the next morning for breakfast. Room service was not called again. The day after the encounter, a maid entered the room to change the sheets, and she found the woman dead in the bathtub with its pinkish-red water. The housekeeper ran from the room screaming down to the lobby. The woman had apparently killed herself after her boyfriend had not shown up that week for their rendezvous.

Other than the elicit affairs hotels often see, the other dark secret that hotels hold is that they are one of the most frequent sites chosen for suicides. There are multiple reasons for this. One is the nature of the clientele. Often the guests travel alone for a living and are more prone to feeling disconnected from the world and succumb to depression. Another is that by committing suicide in a hotel, this saves their family from having to discover them hanging in the basement or lying in the living room with a used revolver at their feet. Hotels don't exactly advertise this in their brochures, but this is one of the primary reasons that so many historic hotels are abundant with tales of ghosts and phantoms.

Room 711 seems to be a room still haunted by this woman's death. Ghost enthusiasts often travel trying to stay in specifically haunted rooms, hoping for an experience while there. Many have attempted this with room 711, but often have not been able to stay the night. It appears that 711's ghost still wants to keep the room to herself. If the room is occupied, she will attempt to disrupt their stay until they leave. It's not uncommon for guests to check out of the room in the middle of the night without an explanation.

Others have seen her on the seventh floor roaming the halls. Rooms 704, 705, and 709 also have resulted in panicked phone calls to the hotel operator.

A story related by one of the clerks occurred in 2004. The young man, a college student at nearby MTSU, worked at the hotel on weekends and weeknights. Over the school year working the front desk there, he had become accustomed to the complaints about room 711, but there was one evening that stuck out in his mind in particular.

A businesswoman in her thirties had checked in at the desk. He recalled her to have been a no-nonsense type of lady. She had a litany of requests involving her stay, including messages and wake-up calls. She had the air of someone who, if inspired, would delight in tearing him to shreds. Whatever business she was in, he suspected she rarely heard, "no." The woman was given the guestroom 711. As she walked to the elevator, her expensive heels clacking with authority, the clerk thought briefly of the room's ghost story. *I bet that ghost doesn't mess with her,* he thought as a smirk appeared in the corner of his mouth. He was wrong.

The woman had entered the room and inspected it briefly. It was acceptable. She began to unpack. She planned on being there for days, so she filled the closets and drawers with her belongings. Feeling the grime of a day spent in an airplane, she went into the bathroom to take a highly anticipated shower. She tossed her dirty travel clothes into the corner and laid her toiletry bag on the counter top. Always the type to plan ahead, she hung a hotel issued robe and towel on a nearby hook, so as not to drip on the floor when she left the tub. She stepped into what would have been a scalding hot shower for most. The businesswoman stood under the water, letting the water rain down on her face. She stayed in the shower for a lengthy time, mentally mapping out the rest of her itinerary in Nashville.

Finally, she turned off the water with pruny fingers. The bathroom billowed with steam like a fog. Her hand slipped from the shower curtain reaching for the towel and robe, but they weren't there. *Did they fall to the ground?* She pulled back the curtain, but the floor was empty. She assumed she had somehow forgotten to hang the towel there and stepped out onto the tile with wet feet. The woman pulled another fresh towel from a chrome rack over the toilet. She dried off and wrapped a towel around her body. She reached for the hairdryer in her toiletry bag, but it wasn't there.

Now *that* she hadn't forgotten. Her head snapped toward the bathroom door. It was still closed, which she had done so she wouldn't freeze when she got out. Possibilities raced through her mind. A hotel thief? A prank? Some kind of voyeur? Her own forgetfulness? A calculating and steely person by nature, she considered and discarded each theory like someone selecting that day's wardrobe. If someone had entered, the cold air from the adjoining room would have sucked the steam from the bathroom. So what was the answer? She didn't know.

She couldn't rule out the possibility that someone else was in her room with one hundred percent certainty. What could she do? She couldn't just stay in the bathroom all night. If someone was outside the door, which she doubted, she might as well get it over with and face it. She looked in the corner for her clothes (if there *was* some dangerous person out there, she would certainly be at a disadvantage with only a towel), but they were gone. She felt a mixture of irritation and uncertainty. The uncertainty was the most annoying. She did not care for the unknown.

She looked around briefly for anything that might serve as a weapon, and saw nothing more threatening than a miniature shampoo bottle. With remarkable calm, she opened the door. The remaining steam blew into the room in a puff and disappeared.

"Is anyone there?" she called out.

No one answered.

After a few seconds, she stuck her head out looking in both directions. No one was there. She started to feel a little foolish for talking to an empty room. She searched the main area of the room, but it was empty. The chair that had held her Burberry purse was gone. She looked at her dresser for the jewelry and watch she had taken off, and it was also empty. Her heart was pounding, more from the anger of feeling violated by this thievery than fear.

*I'm going to rip that front desk clerk's head off, and then the manager is going to get it too. What kind of security is this?* She was thinking these thoughts to herself, when she opened the drawer to get dressed. It was empty, completely wiped out. She went to the wardrobe, and the empty hangers dangled in front of her. Everything was gone. She was furious now. Jewelry and money was one thing, but her business suits and shoes would take a long time to replace. If she had to march down there in her towel she would, and...

Turning to the door, she saw her luggage stacked in a neat little pile. She walked slowly to the bags and picked them up. They were heavy. *What is going on?* She looked around the empty room again, and then carried two of the larger bags back to the bed. With a heave she tossed them on top of the bedspread. Her thumbs popped the locks, and she opened the first bag. Blouses, underwear, books, shoes, nightgowns, and other clothing were all folded neatly into the suitcase. Quickly, she opened the second bag, and it too was full of her belongings.

She ran to the other luggage and searched them. Her purse, a hang-up garment bag, and her toiletry kit were also full. Even her jewelry, watch and wallet were all in her purse. *This room is haunted,* the thought sprung into her mind, and she didn't doubt it. With her mouth hanging open slightly, the woman turned in a slow circle almost as if she was trying to see what could not be seen. She rolled the idea of this being a haunted room over in her mind, and although she didn't previously believe or disbelieve in the idea of ghosts, the impossibility of what had occurred only made this notion seem more plausible.

She got dressed, loaded her bags on a cart in the hall, and went to the clerk at the desk.

It was clear to the young man dressed in his tie and nametag that the woman approaching him was none too happy. "I don't know what's going on with that room, but I either want a refund or a new room," she barked.

In the past he had had people request to leave the room in fright, but this was the only time he had a guest upset with him for not warning her before hand of the room's specter.

He listened to her unload on him and he did not deny her suspicions. "Yes, ma'am, I am sorry. We occasionally get complaints about that room. I would be happy to move you to another suite."

She took him up on his offer to change rooms, and even surprising herself, slept easily that night.

# 14

# Murder in Printer's Alley

istoric Printer's Alley runs between Third and Fourth avenues just off Church Street in the heart of downtown Nashville. The nickname is due to the fact that printing has always been one of the prime industries in the city, and in the early days that area housed many of the city's printing presses. During the sweltering months of summer, the presses would escalate the heat, so the printers could often be seen taking breaks in the alley to cool off. The sight of dozens of printers laughing and carousing is why the alleyway became known as Printer's Alley. Even though the area has evolved and changed a number of times over the years, the nickname has persevered.

Since that time Printer's Alley has had the unfortunate, albeit deserved reputation for violence and crime. In the late 1800s, there were over ninety different brothels in the downtown area and Nashville had a reputation for very high venereal disease rates due to this. There were two major reasons for this type of business thriving in the city. One is that Nashville was a major military port. The other is that after the Civil War there were many widows unable to support themselves. Many women turned to the business of prostitution to survive.

Many viewed the Red Light district as a blemish on the city and were glad when prohibition laws were passed. Most of the saloons around town were closed and many were demolished during this era. The saloons of Printer's Alley were spared because they were under police protection by the mayor. This is why this block holds some of the oldest buildings on that side of town. Local lawyers, businessmen, and politicians would frequent the gambling dens, brothels, and speak-easies in the alley. When a local reporter asked the mayor at the time whether or not he supported the

During prohibition a variety of speak easies, brothels, and underground gambling dens thrived in Printer's Alley. Bootleggers smuggled whiskey in tunnels underneath the streets.

businesses in the alley, he was famously quoted, "Protect them? I patronize them."

Ironically, there had never been a single documented case of homicide in Printer's Alley until prohibition. This introduced organized crime to the area. Nashville was a bootlegging port for Al Capone, who himself often stayed in Nashville on business. Many of the murders that happened during that time were reported to be turf wars between various criminals.

During the 1950s and 1960s, the alley was a great late-night spot for live country music. After the *Grand Ole Opry* would let out a few blocks away, many of the performers like Hank Williams and Dolly Parton would play great midnight shows. From the 1970s through the 1980s, the alley had a reputation for violence, but starting in the early 1990s Nashville worked to revitalize the area. They ran out most of the seedier establishments, opening the area to blues, karaoke, and country western music venues.

Printer's Alley today is an off-the-path tourist attraction for its French architecture reminiscent of New Orleans' French Quarter, country and rock music history, and its famously violent past.

As one walks down the narrow alley passing gaudy neon lights, reverberating guitars, barkers jostling for customers, and women of questionable morals, there stands a century-old building. The remaining frame of an electric sign hangs twenty feet over the cobblestone path below. Boarded up windows and a cobweb covered doorway draw only a cursory glance from the alley's patrons. Only a few locals remember that this abandoned nightclub was the site of one of Nashville's most famous and tragic murders when it was known as the Rainbow Room. It was located on the bottom level of a much larger building with a remarkable history. When first opened in the 1890s, the Southern Turf was considered the finest saloon and brothel in Nashville and catered to the city's most elite gentlemen. The Southern Turf was just doors away from similar establishments like the appropriately named Utopia Hotel and Climax Theatre. In the early 1900s, this row of buildings on 4th Avenue (back then it was called Cherry Street) was known as the Men's District for its cigar shops, billiards, and upscale saloons.

These other locations paled in comparison to the grandeur of the Southern Turf. The Turf was decorated with tropical plants, mahogany wood, rare art, bronze statues, racing prints, and large mirrors. They served imported cigars and boasted an unparalleled wine list. The ladies' rooms upstairs were eventually equipped with secret passageways in case the police ever raided them. Today, a law firm owns the building. The joke amongst locals is that the business hasn't really changed that much there over the years.

Skull Shullman worked at and owned a variety of nightclubs in Printer's Alley from the 1930s until his murder in 1998. In interviews he rarely talked about his early years in the alley. He did once tell of a gambling den at which he worked. The room had green felt tables all around, but was missing the "lines" that would indicate that they were used for various gambling games. When the lights above the tables were turned on, the lines would appear on the tables below. This way, if they were tipped that the police were coming, they could flip off the lights and the tables would transform into "innocent" looking surfaces. Other than this small anecdote, there is little information about his early years there, which has led to speculation about his connections to organized crime.

Nationally, Shullman was famous for a recurring role on a TV show called "Hee Haw." On the show he could usually be seen in the background wearing farmer's coveralls and a silver, skull-shaped belt buckle. He always had a couple of dogs on leashes with him as well. He had been given the role on the show as a token of gesture for introducing many of the cast members to the producer.

Skull continued to dress that way off the show as well, with the coveralls and belt buckle. He was a fixture of downtown in his get-up, walking around with a "Hee Haw" clock resting oddly on the bill of his cap and several dogs on leashes. He dressed this way largely so that he could be recognized for his part on "Hee Haw," using that to lure fans into his establishments. Skull was a huge animal lover and always seemed to have several poodles with him. Their fur would be dyed different colors, like blue, red, or green. By all accounts, Skull Shullman was an eccentric man who often drew curious looks from passersby. Personal opinions

The Southern Turf was the most upscale of all of the saloons and was frequented by Nashville's most powerful men.

about him vary greatly. Some have described him as cruel and vindictive while others have spoken of how generous he could be with his money, often giving cash to the homeless or struggling musicians.

One of Skull Shullman's flaws was that he always carried large amounts of cash on him. This led to a few muggings throughout his life. Skull shared one such story about a robbery that occurred five years before his death. A man was beating him up in a robbery attempt. The thief landed blow after blow. Between punches, Skull looked up at the man and made eye contact. The thief's jaw dropped. Skull later laughed about how the man had recognized him from "Hee Haw" and was star-struck. The thief exclaimed he was a big fan of Skull's, and that he was very sorry to have to rob him but he really needed the money. Unbelievably, the man continued to beat up Shullman and stole his money, despite being a "big fan."

Whatever flaws Skull may have had, he didn't deserve his fate. His death occurred at one of the Alley's better-known clubs, the Rainbow Room.

On the afternoon of Sunday, January 21, 1998, two drifters planned a robbery. They were aware that Skull was a wealthy man. One of the men stood out front watching nervously for anyone who might come by while the other man slid inside. Skull was tending the bar alone. The man rushed Skull demanding he turn over the register. Unfortunately, Skull fought back and a struggle ensued. Both men tumbled about the bar of the Rainbow room in an awkward, violent dance. They crashed into the side of the bar, shattering tumblers and bottles everywhere. Clutched in each other's grasp, the thief reached for a piece of broken glass. He grabbed it and attacked Skull Shullman, slitting his throat. Gasping for air and clawing helplessly at the wound, Skull Shullman slumped to the ground. The thief cleaned out the register and left. When he exited the bar, he and his partner took off in different directions, planning to meet up later.

A few hours later, a cigarette vendor came into the Rainbow Room and saw the broken glasses and the opened register. The vendor's eyes scanned the room and came upon Skull's body on

The front door to the Rainbow Room — and the site of the murder of *Hee Haw* star Skull Shullman.

the floor. He ran over to the man. Skull still had a pulse, but just barely. The vendor called the police and waited.

An ambulance whisked Skull away to the hospital. That evening, his friend, Tammy Wynnette, sang to him at his bedside. He did not survive the night. Skull Shullman was eighty years old at the time of his death.

The story made national headlines and was featured on "America's Most Wanted," due to Skull's fame. There weren't any eyewitnesses, and speculation about Skull's murderer was rampant. Skull had made many enemies in business over the years, leading most to believe that he was targeted.

Despite countless hours of investigation by the police, the trail ran cold. The murder had been considered by most to be forever unsolved. It appeared that Skull's killers would never be identified.

But five years later, one of the men was arrested in Nebraska on a completely separate charge. During the intensity of the interrogation, the man broke down. He confessed to a variety of crimes that he had committed in his life, including the murder of Skull Shullman. He later turned on his partner, and that man was also subsequently arrested. Both men were eventually tried and convicted on a number of accounts, including Skull's murder. They were each given the death penalty. Their names were Jason Spence and James Caveye.

Since that grisly murder, the Rainbow Room has been closed. The interior is a shadowy resemblance of its past with broken furniture, mildewed signed headshots of various entertainers, and layers of dust covering everything. Although no one has leased the room since, it's been used as a makeshift storage building by the Blues bar next door. The Blues Club would keep items that weren't needed on a daily basis like extra chairs, tables, or cases of glasses in the empty club.

Over time, the staff began having inexplicable episodes. The bar-backs would often enter the storage room alone to fetch a keg or case of napkins. On some occasions, they would claim to hear whispers from all around. They would spin in circles trying to spy the source, but the room would prove empty. If an employee would happen to cross the part of the floor where Skull's body was found, he would often feel severe coldness, even though the room itself was very hot and stuffy. Cold spots are a common symptom of haunted locations. Some of the witnesses described seeing a dark, shadow figure crossing the room, although no actual person was there. It was frequently reported that a sweet smell could be picked up in the air, like Aqua Velva or Stetson. Skull was famous for his cheap colognes.

On a particular evening a couple of years after Shullman's murder, one of the bar backs from the Blues Club entered the old Rainbow Room to retrieve a rack of glasses. The room was dark, but he knew the layout and where he was going. This hulking man with long red hair crossed the floor and knelt like a weight lifter to pick up the heavy glasses. Just as he was about to lift, he felt a hand plop down on his right shoulder. He spun around half expecting a fight, but no one was there. That night he told the manager that from now on he would only go inside if he had a partner with him. His manager found it amusing that such a large man would need an escort anywhere.

Over the years a variety of ghost hunters have claimed to have captured Skull on film. Most of the pictures of him have been taken at the doorway entering the Rainbow Room. The photographs themselves are always clear, but to the right of the door often a bright cloud emerges. It appears that the face of Skull Shullman is inside this multicolored cloud burst. It's logical that he chose to materialize in this location because in life he was known to sit on a little folding chair in this spot taking money at the door with his poodles all around his feet.

# 15

# The Savage House

J ust a few steps off the beaten Broadway path on a quiet street stands a Victorian treasure. The Savage House, built in the 1840s, is one of only two pre-Civil War homes still standing in downtown Nashville. This glorious townhouse fashioned from pink brick with large cream painted wooden windows stands proudly among the modern buildings that surround her. The ornate details of the home and quaint courtyard in back are reminiscent of a historic New Orleans neighborhood.

Through the years, the home has seen many residents come and go. This grand building was originally a boarding house to some of Nashville's most well known citizens. In later years, it was home to a Jewish men's club originally called the Concordia Society Club. Upon moving into the house, the club's name was changed to "The Standard." The Standard Club made a few interesting changes to the home in 1883. They added a new building in the rear, which housed a large ballroom on the upper level. The lower level was made into a professional style bowling alley and is said to be one of the earliest in Nashville.

In 1898, Dr. and Mrs. Giles C. Savage purchased the building. Savage, a professor of ophthalmology at Vanderbilt, ran his medical practice and recovery hospital from the basement and the first floor. The magnificent free-floating, wooden staircase led to the second and third floors, which remained exclusive to the family and their guests. In the early 1980s, the building was purchased and made into a Bed and Breakfast, and the section of the house that was once Dr. Savage's office was turned into a tearoom. Some of the employees and regulars at the tearoom believe that Dr. Savage has never left.

**One of the oldest remaining homes in downtown Nashville, the Savage House is haunted by a little girl on the third floor.**

A few years ago, a server at the tearoom recalled an unforgettable experience. It was late after his shift, and he and the owner were going about the regular set of chores involved in closing for the night. The server was alone in the back parlor, busy clearing the dishes from his tables and preparing to take them back to kitchen, when he caught a glimpse of a person out of the corner of his eye. Startled, he whipped around losing his balance and dropped a fork onto the floor. Instinctively, he bent down quickly to pick up the utensil. He slowly rose from the floor only to find that he was alone in the room. "That was odd," he thought to himself, "What a long day, I need to get home and get some rest." Walking back to the kitchen, he passed the owner and smiled as if to say that he would be finished soon. Weary, the server walked back to the parlor and was shocked to find a man sitting at the table next to the bay window. The man was dressed in a Victorian style black suit and hat. The server began to approach the gentleman when he realized the stranger was

The entrance to the Savage House.

*TRANSPARENT.* Frightened, the server gasped for air making a loud sound that captured the attention of the man in black. When he turned around, the server discovered that the man, who judging by his clothing was clearly from another era, had *no face.* Under his hat, in the shape of a head, was a dark cloudy mist. At the sight of the faceless man, the server ran into the kitchen to get the owner of the tearoom. Reluctantly, the owner walked into the parlor area to find that there was no one in the dining area. Chalking it up to exhaustion, the server convinced himself that he was simply seeing things.

Weeks later, the server was introduced to a previous employee of the tearoom who had come back for a visit. He remarked on how nothing had changed and how comforting it was to be back. The server invited the gentleman to stay after closing time and enjoy some cocktails with the remaining staff. Several hours and many drinks later, the workers and the guest were enjoying stories of past customers and happenings at their business. The conversation flowed as if they had all been friends for years. During a pause, the server saw his opportunity to ask if anyone had anything unusual happen in the building. "As a matter of fact," said the guest, "I had weird things happen all the time when I worked here. Once I had a chair that wouldn't stay tucked under the table. No matter how many times I put it back, when I would turn around it would be sitting right out next to the table again. Then I figured it out..."

"Figured what out?" the server interrupted.

"I figured out that when the ghost was finished looking out the window, he would put it back on his own."

"What ghost?" the server said with anticipation.

"The man in black," he started, "You know, the one without a face. You mean you haven't seen him?"

Excited, the server shared his story with the entire group only to find that he and the guest were not the only two who had witnessed the apparition. Two other servers at the table came forward with similar stories of the well-dressed faceless man. Walking by, the owner of the tearoom caught a bit of the conversation. He added, "When we first opened here a lady claiming to be a psychic was having lunch, and when I stopped by to ask her about her meal, she told me that we have two ghosts in the building. I just sort of laughed it off, but she did mention an older gentleman haunting the tearoom. She said he was dressed in all black. You know at the turn of the century doctors dressed all in black, so maybe Mr. Savage has come back for a visit too."

"The lady mentioned two ghosts," the server started almost afraid to finish his sentence, "Who's the other ghost?"

The owner began, "Well, I haven't had a run in with her yet, but some of my guests at the bed and breakfast claimed to have seen her. The psychic said that her name was Myra, and she mostly hangs around the third floor."

Relieved, the server declared, "Well, I guess I will never visit the third floor. I'll just stick down here with old faceless Savage."

The owner went on to tell the story of young Myra on floor number three. He had quite a few guests mention seeing a little girl around the age of ten with nut-brown hair in long pin curls and big magnetic eyes.

"One of my regular renters said that Myra loved to move his watch from the dresser to the nightstand. He usually didn't see her in his room. Mostly people say that they see her in this little room at the top of the stairs."

"Why do you think this child is haunting the manor?" questioned one of the interested listeners.

"You know, I am not sure why she is here, or even who she is, but I do know that from the stories I have heard that she loves to cause a lot of mischief by moving stuff and opening and closing drawers. My guess is that she lived here as a child, when it was a boarding house and maybe died tragically, but I don't really know," he stated.

The server, who seemed too frightened to go on, asked in a sarcastic tone, "So what *do* you know then?"

The owner, who had begun to walk away, turned around with a smile and said, "Well, I know that I don't really believe in all the ghost stuff. I've never seen either one of them and I am here alone all the time. But we did have a second psychic stop by the restaurant last week, and he told me that we had two ghosts in this building. One was a man in black and the other, well her name is Myra."

# 16

# The Tragedy of Georgia and Charlie

erchant's Restaurant on Broadway downtown has been operating since 1988, but the building's history is much more storied than its diners might suspect.

The three-story building opened in 1870. The bottom floor held a pharmacy, the second floor was a hardware manufacturing company, and the third floor was a wholesale drug company. The pharmacy on the first floor had a marble counter top, and one could often find children huddled around it eating ice cream. Some of the popular ice cream sodas sold there contained opiates such as cocaine. Eventually laws were passed banning the sale of these desserts on Sunday hence without the soda the treats were called 'sundaes.'

In 1892, the building was transformed into a boarding house. For the price of twenty-five cents a day, a traveling merchant or soldier could spend the night. An additional quarter could buy the guest a meal. It eventually became one of the city's many brothels and during Prohibition was a speak-easy associated with Al Capone.

During the 1890s, there was a well-known love affair between Georgia Edmondson and Charlie Keenan. Charlie was a soldier who often stayed at the boarding house and Georgia worked for Merchant's. Their turbulent romance has been recorded and preserved in a series of love letters between the two. The restaurant has saved these and displays them in frames throughout the building.

It's not known in what capacity Georgia worked at Merchant's. Some have speculated that she was a "working girl" and that Charlie was one of her customers. Other less cynical readers of the letters have thought differently. Regardless, it's clear through their notes that they were deeply in love with each other.

**The tragic love affair of Georgia and Charlie is preserved in hand-written letters the two wrote each other.**

Eventually Charlie was unfaithful to her, and Georgia broke off the relationship. The letters indicate Charlie's torment. He wanted to see her and make amends face to face. Stationed far away, he was unable to return and Georgia quit sending him letters. Finally Charlie made his way back to Nashville to repair the damage he had caused. The people at Merchant's told him that Georgia was gone and had been so for at least a year. They had no idea to where she had moved on.

Devastated, Charlie checked into a room on the top floor and hung himself.

Today, the staff at Merchant's believe him to still be there searching for his beloved Georgia. Many have seen a soldier wandering about the building, looking for his lost love. On the bottom floor, someone has carved on a storage room door the words "Charlie's Room." Several employees have mentioned feeling uncomfortable there. The strangest aspect of the room is that no matter what the temperature in the rest of the building, Charlie's room is always cold. It's especially cool in the center of the room.

# 17

# The Morgue

D uring the Civil War, several churches and homes around Nashville were used as hospitals for injured soldiers. One building in the downtown Nashville area in particular was used as a morgue. Before the Civil War, the building was owned by William Stockel, who sold cement, firebricks, terra cotta, fire clay, plaster of Paris, doors, windows, and columns. Nashville was badly hit in a variety of battles during the war and fatalities were at astonishing numbers.

The building today holds the Ernest Tubb Record Shop on one side and a famed honky tonk called Crossroads on the other. The Crossroads side was previously used for Confederate corpses and the Ernest Tubb Record shop side was designated for the Union's fallen. There were so many bodies coming through both sides of the morgue that they eventually were equipped with a pulley system resembling a dumb waiter contraption, so that they could more efficiently lower the high volume of bodies into the basement.

Both the record store and bar have been investigated by professional ghost hunters and have reportedly had readings "off the charts." The employees seem to agree.

One former bartender at Crossroads said she had to leave because of the crazy things that would happen there. After closing time, bartenders often are the last to leave, cleaning for hours afterward. This particular bartender recalled a night where she had been closing down the bar.

It had been a busy night and everything was in disarray. She meticulously faced the labels of the hundred or so liquor bottles on the shelves behind the bar. She explained how this was important to bartenders, so that when it's busy they can quickly

**Some investigators believe the building holding the Ernest Tubb Record Shop to be the most haunted in Nashville. It served as a Civil War morgue.**

find the bottle they need. The bartender finished facing all of the bottles and took the trash out to the dumpster. When she returned minutes later, the bottles were all turned in a variety of sporadic directions.

This had not been the first — or the last experience — she had with the building's ghost. It was a few weeks later that she quit. Unable to deal with the ghosts, she took another bartending gig that made less money simply to avoid the stress of the buildings darker presence.

The Ernest Tubb Record Shop has also confirmed a difficulty in retaining employees. For many years the store was the site of a radio program named "The Midnight Jamboree." After the *Grand Ole Opry* would let out nearby, "The Midnight Jamboree" would follow at the shop. Shoulder to shoulder, fans would watch their favorite singers perform in the back of the room. Loretta Lynn famously would stand on a Coca-Cola crate so that people in the back could see her. The Ernest Tubb Record Shop boasts an unrivaled selection of country music albums and displays many items of memorabilia and bluegrass history.

Besides the autographs and glass-encased costumes, the store has held onto other aspects of the past more spiritual in nature. Clerks are often reluctant to go to the downstairs area in particular. Cold spots and the pervasive feeling of being watched are widely reported.

The most unusual experiences involve the store's CD player. Often, if in the middle of a conversation while browsing through the store someone says, "I wish they'd play Hank Williams," or "I'm looking for Chet Atkins," for example, the artist named is the next musician that is played in the store's CD player. This seems to occur even if the CD player hasn't been programmed previously to do so.

# 18

# Hume-Fogg

## Sibling Rivalry

I
n 1855, Nashville's first public school, Hume High School, opened its doors; twenty years later, Fogg High School opened next door in 1875. In 1912, both schools were combined into a new building, Hume-Fogg, which still stands today. It's now a magnet school for Nashville and has educated distinguished alumni such as singer Dinah Shore and pin-up queen and salutatorian of her class, Bettie Page. Students often talk favorably of their experience at the school. Impromptu field trips are common due to the museums, historic landmarks, library, and music halls within walking distance of the school.

On Broadway, the school rests atop a hill just a few blocks from the Cumberland River. It appears more like a medieval castle than a school to passersby. The classrooms are enormous and the inside of the structure can be confusing to the unfamiliar. There are a variety of "secret passages" and routes to get around the school, and several areas are off limits to the studentbody.

The most fascinating area is beneath the school building where there is a twisting and damp network of tunnels. Standing water, rusted pipes, fallen walls, long abandoned lockers, debris, and filth of all kind can be found in the dark labyrinth. Many a student has gotten lost down there on a variety of mischievous excursions. One of the rooms in the building was once used as a small police station, and beneath the officers' feet, a bootlegger's tunnel ran down to the river undiscovered for many years.

There have been a few ghost stories about the building passed down over the years from the senior classes to the wide-eyed

**Hume-Fogg is rumored to have been the site of a grisly murder between two jealous brothers.**

incoming freshmen, which have been confirmed by alumni. Many believe that Confederate ghosts haunt the building. Near the cafeteria, students have claimed witness to bloodied and bandaged soldiers sitting in the courtyard nearby. Another female alum told a story of her years there in the 1970s. She said that one afternoon her class was walking in single file down the hall with the squeaking sound of sneakers filling the air. The front of the line stopped and the trickle effect was that each succeeding student stopped. Some who had their heads turned whispering to those behind them in line walked into the stalled student in front of them. Eventually everyone stopped, and the witness in the back of the line recalled that the sound of their shoes squeaking had ceased.

But she could still hear the sound of boots on the floor. She said that it was a rhythmic, marching sound, as if a platoon of infantrymen were marching through the halls.

The most widespread story involves a fatal sibling rivalry. The story has been passed down for generations and some of the details and names vary slightly depending on who is asked. The most common version of the story is that sometime around 1915 two brothers attended the school. The older brother had a girlfriend and discovered that his younger brother was seeing her behind his back.

There used to be a swimming pool on the bottom level of the school and it's said that he confronted his brother by the pool. Before anyone could step in, both brothers fell into the water clawing and swinging at each other as they hit the water. Water splashed everywhere, and the other students stood frozen watching the two brothers thrashing wildly in the pool. Once, the younger brother's face emerged from the water coughing and gasping before going back under. Finally, the older brother burst to the surface coughing and swimming frantically for the edge of the pool. His brother did not come up, and a few boys jumped into the water, diving toward his body that was sinking limply toward the bottom. It was too late.

After a difficult effort, they pulled him to the pool's ladder. The other boys slid him onto the concrete surface. His face and eyes were lifeless. One student ran for a teacher. The older brother sat feet away on the ground, feeling the first pangs of loss and regret as the rage faded. The pool was closed a few years later, floored over with concrete, but the story has not been as easily covered....

Time has clouded the story. Sometimes it's told involving twin brothers. Others say it was an accidental drowning, not involving a girl at all. Some don't believe the event *ever* occurred. Whatever the true story, the years since have produced a common result. Many students have reported that while on the bottom level they can still hear water splashing underneath the concrete. This occurs even though there is not any running water beneath the floor.

Some have even said that while standing there listening to the splashing water, without warning they would be startled by a pounding sound underneath the floor. It's as if someone is trapped on the underside, pounding with their fist trying to escape. It seems unlikely that he ever will.

# 19

## Past Perfect

On the south side of Broadway, this area of downtown Nashville used to be mostly industrial in nature. Auto repair, salvage shops, printers, and junkyards were the types of less aesthetically appealing businesses in the area. As the downtown district has grown, it has started to expand into the industrial side of the city. The Country Music Hall of Fame, Hilton Hotel, luxury condos, and the Schermerhorn Symphony Hall have all been erected in recent years.

Some of the older buildings have found new life as more urban businesses have moved in that cater to the new feel of the area. One such restaurant and bar is known as Past Perfect in a century-old brick building. The location had seen a number of businesses over the years including the Greer and Blanton Wagon Co., a furniture store, a grocery, and mostly machinists. The three owners from Chicago have decades of combined experience in the service industry. In the winter of 2006, they opened their restaurant featuring their own culinary creations and an extensive wine list. Located next to the symphony hall, they soon found their niche as a place to dine before the shows and are also one of the few downtown restaurants that serve food well past midnight.

After the first year, they realized the risk they had taken in their investment was a success. However, it didn't come easily. There were complications in advertising, competition, staffing, location, and countless other challenges, but the most surprising one was that the restaurant was *HAUNTED*.

In 2006, while one of the owners stayed back in Chicago tying up loose ends, the other two owners, Sean and Matt, began the arduous task of opening the store—and it wasn't long before they had suspicious activity in the restaurant.

**Past Perfect's ghost can be heard walking throughout the upper floor.**

They spent day and night preparing the bistro for their grand opening, and on more than one occasion, they believed they were not alone. They would hear the footsteps of someone coming from the storage room. Curious, one of the owners would peek into the dry storage room. It would be empty. Although it was a little strange, this type of event was always dismissed as a figment of their imagination or decided to be a sound from outside.

It happened repeatedly over the following weeks. The sound always seemed to come from either the storage room or the balcony seating upstairs. The noise always brought about the image of heavy work boots shuffling across the floor. This alone did not raise any thoughts about ghosts, but other events did.

The name, Past Perfect, for the restaurant refers to the historic décor of the interior. Dozens of old maps, black and white photographs, signs, and antique imagery give the guests a feeling of stepping into the past, an irony not lost on those aware of the building's haunting.

One of the co-owners, Matt, was meticulous in the way that he hung all of the pictures and memorabilia. With much deliberation, he carefully placed each picture frame, taking all afternoon and evening to complete the task. The other owner, Sean, teased him a bit about it.

The next day, Sean and Matt entered the bar and immediately could see that someone had been there. Each and every one of the paintings and pictures were off of their hooks. They were laying face down on the ground below where Matt had placed them the day before. Irritated, Matt turned to Sean and accused him of doing this as some kind of joke. Sean laughed and denied it.

Everything else seemed untouched. Months later, Sean still denied removing the pictures.

The strangeness didn't stop after the restaurant opened. The phenomenon also wasn't exclusive to the owners. At closing time, a female bartender and a waitress confirmed what is believed to be the first sighting of the building's ghost. The bartender was downstairs while the waitress was on the balcony level placing silverware rolls on the cleaned tables. Near the balcony's black railing, the bartender saw a dark shadowy figure standing there. She screamed out to the waitress, and the waitress shouted back, also seeing the black, human shape just ten feet away from her.

"Do you see that?"

"Yes!"

"What is it?"

"I don't know!"

They shouted this type of excited exchange back and forth in a rapid-fire manner. The figure moved toward the staircase. They both screamed, feeding off of each other's hysteria.

The black shadow seemed alive, and the bartender watched in horror as it approached the steps that led down to the dining area, and, even worse, toward her. Living shadow ghosts like this are known as "black aggies" in many areas of the country, but they didn't know this. They only knew that they wanted desperately to not be seeing what they were seeing.

The shadow stopped at the top of the stairs, stayed there for a moment, and then faded away.

They also claimed to have seen a man seated at a table upstairs, hunched over like a man playing cards. Upon approach, he disappears.

Over the first few weeks of Past Perfect's opening, the other owner, Sean, began to hear his name called.

"Sean," a hushed tone would call out. Sean would turn casually around to see who it was. No one would be behind him. This occurred over a dozen times with his name being spoken aloud... and each time he was either alone or the other staff seemed busy doing other things.

"Did you call my name?" Sean would ask.

"Hmm? No, not me," the others would always say.

He kept this to himself. Hearing voices wasn't exactly the kind of thing you advertised to people, especially with your employees. One night, the bar was particularly busy, and Sean jumped in to help the bartender. He was pouring beers and shaking martinis at the server's well. Waiters and waitresses were gathered around while they waited on their customer's drinks.

"Sean," the voice whispered. Sean didn't even look up. The voice had almost become part of the scenery to him, like the chatter at the bar or the hum of the ice machine.

"Sean," the voice hushed in the same way once more. Again, he ignored it.

"Hey Sean, I think someone's calling for you." Sean's head popped up and with wide eyes he glared at the server, Chuck, across the bar. Chuck was looking around in a way that suggested he was trying to determine who had called out Sean's name. This was the first time he had been aware that anyone besides himself could hear the voice. This was a relief in a way, knowing he wasn't crazy. It also posed a new problem. Whose voice had he been hearing?

Other employees and diners have also mentioned hearing their names called from seemingly empty space.

These incidents, as well as others, made the owners begin to suspect that the building may have a ghost or two. They approached the landlord and he confirmed their fears. The landlord matter-of-factly described his encounters with the ghost there. Without any knowledge of Sean or Matt's experiences, the landlord's stories were eerily similar.

The landlord used to live in an apartment in the back of the store in what is now the kitchen for Past Perfect. He had a storefront on the street side of the building. At night, he would wake up in his bed to the sound of someone stumbling around in the store.

Cautiously, he would slide into the store from the entrance to his apartment. Long shadows stretched everywhere due to the streetlamps outside. He would creep through the brick building in search of the intruder. Occasionally, he would bump into a display table rattling the items on it. He would grimace knowing he had given away his position in the darkness. He would stand frozen, waiting for someone to jump out at him or bolt for the door. There would only be silence. He continued his search, but never found anything.

This happened continuously and each time he could not find a trespasser or a point of entry. He came to believe that a homeless man was sneaking in at night and squatting there. The landlord eventually purchased a gun, thinking one night the intruder would try to kill him in his sleep. After awhile, it became apparent that there wasn't any *living* person in the store. He carefully locked up each night from within, and after a night of hearing a man stomping around the wooden floors of the store, the next morning's daylight revealed unmoved locks and latches throughout the building.

He came to the same conclusion that Sean and Matt had. The building was haunted. He looked into the history of the building to try and find what might have occurred to cause such strange sounds. At one point the store had been Englert Engine Company, a well-known repair shop for many years. He asked the other business owners if they knew of any murders or accidental deaths that may have happened there in the past; a few of the old-timers recalled one of the repairmen dying on the site of a heart attack.

This seemed like a possible explanation. Maybe this man, who died before his time, was still here—a ghost trapped between life and death.

This offered the staff at least a possible explanation, but there were new manifestations that seemed separate from their ghost. At first they thought this activity was all caused by the same spirit, but after several months it became clear that another presence was seeking attention.

On certain nights, singers and songwriters performed on a small stage in front of the large window facing the street. In the middle of a chorus, the power has turned off inexplicably. Other times when the restaurant was full of dining couples, the overhead lights have turned off with no one near the switch when it happened. One morning, the opening manager found a glass of water had been thrown on a large, old map of Nashville hanging on the wall, smearing some of the ink. The activity by this spirit seemed mischievous in nature and it's now believed to be caused by the ghost of a young girl around ten years of age.

The staff refers to her as "Maria," although it's uncertain how this name came to be known. It could be a nickname, or she may have "spoken" to one of the employees. Some have seen her, mostly downstairs, and she has been captured on film at least once on the steps. The image revealed the petite frame of a young girl with dark hair. Whoever she is and why her spirit is restless is unclear. She's one of the most enigmatic ghosts in the city.

# 20

# Curse of the Bell Witch

The Bell Witch is one of the world's best-known ghost stories. Although the majority of the horrific events involving the Bell Witch occurred in Adams, Tennessee, the story has a strong Nashville connection. Many of the eyewitnesses to the haunting were Nashvillians including Andrew Jackson and many of the descendants of the tormented family involved have lived in the city of Nashville. The Bell Witch herself isn't really a witch at all. She's believed by most to be a ghost, but because of her relentless persecution and the brutal torture she inflicted on the Bell family, she was named the "Bell Witch" during the time of her reign of terror from 1817 to 1821. In those days, anything viewed as unholy or evil was considered witchcraft. Many researchers consider the Bell Witch the only documented case in which a ghost has actually killed a living person.

The legend really begins in Adams, Tennessee, a rural farming community north of Nashville on the Tennessee-Kentucky border. A man named John Bell lived there with his family. He was a well-respected man in local politics and religious circles and seemed hardly the type of person to have deserved the wretched future that he was destined to endure.

John Bell sold a slave to a woman named Kate Batts and an arrangement of payments was made. Months later, Kate disputed the interest rate and sought legal retribution. The courts favored Kate Batts' version of the story and awarded her justly, finding that John Bell was in error.

Vindicated, Kate Batts should have felt content in the court's judgment, but she wasn't. A wealthy, vengeful, and exceptionally moody woman, Kate shared her distaste in John Bell with anyone who would listen. A powerful member of the

Red River Baptist Church, she was successful in having him excommunicated from the congregation. This was painful for John, who was a deeply spiritual man, but he never lost faith in his religion. On numerous occasions, Batts would tell the townspeople of Adams how she would never rest in her quest for revenge against John Bell. Few doubted her promise. It was well known that Kate was a dangerous combination of persistent and crazy. Kate Batts died a month after the excommunication of John Bell from his church.

It seemed that John's conflicts with Kate Batts were over and thoughts of her rarely crossed his mind months later. He had plenty to keep himself busy with his large farm and eight children. The thousand-acre Bell farm was situated on a bluff overlooking the winding Red River below. The land was populated with massive oak trees, wildflowers, and several Indian burial mounds. They farmed a variety of crops, but mostly corn and tobacco. They lived a relatively simple, if not picturesque, life.

One particular warm late afternoon in 1817, John was making his way back from the fields toward the Bell's family log cabin home. His clothes were covered with dirt and he wiped at the sweat on his brow with his calloused hands. Not far from the cabin, John stopped walking and sensed something in the cornrow to his right. Calmly, he turned his head toward the corn so as to not startle whatever animal was there.

The black hair on the creature made it almost invisible in the first row of corn where it was sitting. At first John thought it was a dog and tried to determine if it was friendly or not. He stepped a foot forward to get a better look and stopped. The creature released a guttural sound that was more akin to rumbling thunder than that of a dog.

Bell's heart was pounding immediately. Mentally, he fought the urge to run to the cabin, knowing that this would only spook the dog. He focused on trying to stay calm and alert to any movement from the...well, what was it exactly? The closer he looked at the dog, the less it looked like one. It was the height of a canine, but it was not of any breed he had seen before. Short, black coarse hair covered the animal's body and its considerable muscles seemed to ripple underneath its fur with each heavy breath it took. Its ears were long and its nose twitched like the beast might sneeze any second. Its mouth seemed to hold dozens of jagged and menacing teeth. Huge strings of drool dripped from the corners of its fanged mouth, falling into sickening pools at its enormous feet.

As slowly as he could manage, John started sidestepping toward the front porch of the cabin. He never took his eyes off the animal, which slowly watched John make his way to the front door with its charcoal eyes. On the porch, the wood beneath his feet creaked and groaned, intensifying his terror with each noise. The animal never moved, only watching him in its almost curious manner.

At the open front door, John reached in the frame with his left arm grabbing blindly for his rifle he prayed was still there. He dared not break eye contact with the mongrel. His fingers touched the cool steel of his rifle propped against the doorway. In a swift motion, he had the weapon mounted on his shoulder and aimed on the black animal not twenty feet away in the corn. The creature just stared back at him, almost daring him to fire. John took a step forward, now feeling confident with his gun in hand. The sound of the gun's blast rang out, scaring a flock of previously unseen crows to take to the air from behind the cornstalks.

The animal stared blankly at John for several seconds. *That's not possible! How did I miss?* John lowered the gun and watched as the black creature slowly rose from its haunches and turned nonchalantly into the rows of corn.

John reloaded the rifle as quickly as he could and followed. It was too dangerous to let the creature live with so many of his little ones playing all about the farm. The dog-like animal had walked casually into the field, meaning it couldn't be far. John waded into the stalks determined to hunt down the thing and kill it.

Fifteen minutes later, he reemerged with his rifle still loaded, as when he had entered before.

That night, he described the experience and learned that his eleven-year-old daughter, Betsy, had also seen the creature in the fields. This was his fear, that the beast could maul the children. He later learned that some of the slaves had also seen the animal that seemed to be part dog and part something else.

Over the next couple of days, John and his wife, Lucy, kept a watchful eye out for the animal, but it never reappeared. They had hoped that the creature had simply wandered on beyond their property.

On another evening soon after, as John and his wife talked with each other in their home, a persistent knocking noise began outside. They ignored it for a moment, but as it got louder John tried to find the source. He was unable to find the cause, and had gone outside suspecting to find one of his children banging the wall with a stick or perhaps a strong wind blowing branches against the house. Outside, John found the air to be perfectly still, almost eerily so. He rounded the house and no children – or black dog-like beasts – were anywhere in sight.

On consecutive nights this occurred disturbing the sleep of all of the children. Knocks, thuds, and bangs all over the house by some mysterious source for months in a row made John and Lucy think that perhaps the stalking beast had been a bad omen. On some nights, the children would swear it sounded like something was gnawing hungrily on the wood outside or running a jagged fingernail across the windows. In the midst of the commotion, John and Lucy began to notice a distant whistling sound. The whistle was faint like a train miles in the distance. Each time, the whistle would be louder and louder. With each occurrence, it seemed that the noise was gaining strength. It sounded less like an artificial whistle, but more human in nature. It was almost as if someone were moaning or crying in some hidden area within the walls.

This was terrifying for the children. Of course, John and Lucy were scared as well, but had to offer a brave face for the little ones. They prayed with the children that the torment would end, but it was of no avail. Publicly, they did not speak of what they were going through. Already excommunicated from the church, the Bells were uncertain what kind of scrutiny they might endure if this were widely known. With each passing month, as the pounding, groaning, and scratching sounds grew, they feared that this would never end. Unfortunately for the Bells, not only did it not end, it also got worse.

Almost a year after the first day that John had seen the black creature in his corn fields, he and Lucy were awakened by the screams of one of their eight children. They each jumped out of bed with their hearts pounding at the horrible sound of one of their own children in fear. They ran out of their bedroom door and stopped, almost falling all over each other. Which child was it? It was Joel, their youngest at four years old. Their stomachs sank.

John and Lucy burst into the room and for a moment were stunned by the sight. Joel was sitting up at the head of his bed with his back to the headboard, and his feet were pulled as close to his body as he could manage. He was screaming and watching his bedding twist and thrash in a violent manner. It was as if the sheets had a mind of their own. They would spin, arch, and flap in a series of random patterns. John ran to him and scooped him up in his protective arms.

Joel shared his room with his slightly older brother, Richard, and Lucy wondered how he could be sleeping through all of this. She looked over at his bed and realized he wasn't sleeping at all. A pillow was on top of his face, and his arms and legs were flailing wildly. *It's killing him! My boy!*

She rushed to Richard's bed and pulled at the pillow. It did not budge. Some impossible force was suffocating her child. She pulled again, and still the pillow did not move. To Lucy's horror, it seemed that Richard was not fighting as strongly as before.

"Let go of him! Please, let him free!" she cried on the edge of hysteria.

The pillow came free with ease. Lucy's pull threw her onto the wooden floors. She sprang back up and clutched Richard with both arms. Richard was coughing for air, and Lucy pulled away and began patting him on the back to try and help him catch his breath. At the doorway she could see her other children standing at the entrance, the older boys trying to comfort their younger sisters and brothers. Their faces were all lost of color.

"John, what have we done to deserve this? What are we going to do?"

John could only shake his head ... he had no answer.

The next night was mercifully uneventful, as was the next, and the next. Weeks passed and it appeared that whatever bedevilment they had encountered had climaxed with the assault on Joel and Richard. They were finally able to rest easier and return to the routine of their lives.

From somewhere in the house, the children began to hear singing. It was distant and hard to make out, but it sounded like a church hymn of some sort. Privately, they feared the worst.

A few nights later, they were awakened again by their child's tortured screams, but this time it wasn't Joel. It was their daughter, Betsy. John and Lucy ran into her room, and found Betsy in bed lying on her back with her arms held out stiffly in front of her. Her cheeks were red and swollen as if she had been beaten, and her head rocked back and forth, like she had been slapped repeatedly by a phantom hand. New welts appeared, and John and Lucy tried to pull her free without success. From somewhere in the background, the sound of a woman's voice swelled. It sounded like a wheezing laugh.

Finally she was free. Her parents jerked their crying daughter from her bed and held her protectively. Their eyes darted all over the room searching for some sign as to the cause of their torment. The sheets on the bed began to swirl, slowly at first, and then they lifted into the air like a small twister. They watched in wonder as the whirlwind of sheets spun faster and faster at rapid speed. They twirled for several seconds before finally losing their power. The white sheets floated innocently to the ground.

Nearly every night this type of activity would occur. Sometimes, furniture would crash to the ground; on other nights they would find Betsy hanging by her hair over the bed. For unknown reasons, the evil force focused most of its energies on John and his daughter Betsy. Lucy was left alone entirely and could only watch helplessly as her husband and daughter were beaten, scratched, and strangled night after night by their unseen assailant.

At first they told no one about their troubles, but the bruises and scratches on the children started to raise the eyebrows of their neighbors. It soon became clear that the nightly visits would not end and that they needed help. John enlisted the aid of a neighboring farmer and friend named James Johnston. He shared his story of the dog, the moving furniture, the crying and laughing sounds, and the beatings they had endured. James listened intently, but believed that the children were pulling some kind of prank.

The Bell family hosted James and his wife for the night. James was unafraid and only agreed to this to placate his friend. They slept in a guest room and John wondered if their dark entity would show itself to strangers. An hour or so later, James and his wife charged into John and Lucy's room. Their eyes were wide and they were panting as if they had just run a mile up hill. Their newly discovered belief in the home's evil presence was all over their faces.

"Some evil demon has entered your house, John Bell. This is the work of the Devil," James said and John only nodded. He could hardly disagree.

James Johnston gathered a group of parishioners to perform an exorcism on the home, but they were unsuccessful. James documented all of the events of the beatings and visits from the witch during the fruitless attempts. Word spread quickly around the countryside about the Bell's troubles. Several of Adams' locals visited the farm, and they confirmed the presence of the dark spirit there. The entity became known as the Bell Witch, although no one was certain if it were a demon, witch, ghost, or a hoax causing the family's tribulations. Many of the visitors to the Bell farm claimed that the trouble followed them home as well. The community in Adams was on the verge of hysteria.

The Bell Witch would cackle, cry, and moan, but no audible words were heard until Reverend Gunn, a distant relative to the Bell clan, at last visited the family. John hoped that the

Reverend's visit might somehow cleanse the home of the evil that had invaded it. In the center of the house, John and Lucy watched desperately as the holy man stood with his arms outstretched and his palms faced up. "Evil spirit," he spoke and swallowed hard before continuing, "Who are you that so tortures and frightens this good man and his family of the Lord? Why have you continued to bring your wrath down on these innocent children and their parents?"

These types of attempts to elicit a response had been tried countless times before without success. John and Lucy, to be honest, didn't really expect much more on this occasion. A silent moment passed, but then...they could hear a wheezing sound, as if the home were taking a breath. A croaking voice of a woman could be heard.

*"I am here to see to it that John Bell is dead for all of his sins, Reverend. I am the witch of Kate Batts that John Bell crossed."*

John's heart sank and his head was spinning. He could feel his hand trembling uncontrollably. *Kate Batts.* He had hardly thought of the woman since she had died over a year ago, but it made some sort of sense. The idea of the being in their home as a ghost had been considered, but the question had always been why. The ghost being that of Kate Batts would explain why she had seemed so vengeful and angry. If this were true, he realized that meant he might be doomed. Because, if the ghost of Kate Batts were anything like the *person named* Kate Batts, then the ghost would not only be relentless and full of bottomless vengeance, but she would also be insane. And insanity could not be reasoned with. With his mind swirling, he only barely noticed when his wife stepped forward.

Lucy looked up with searching eyes toward the ceiling, "Why our children? Why Betsy? They have done nothing to you to deserve such...such..." Her voice cracked and she pulled her hand to her chest unable to say anymore. The Bell Witch did not respond, but only continued its horrible groaning sound for another minute until it petered out completely.

The frightened trio was left standing alone in the room with one mystery solved, but a whole new range of questions were left unanswered.

The event with Reverend Gunn seemed to have given the Bell Witch her voice. This new feature only added to their torment. One thing became clear; the Bell Witch was certainly insane. She spoke frequently to the Bell's with threats and promises. However, sometimes she would leave gifts, like new clothing, if she were pleased with one of the children. She sometimes changed her name, calling herself Black Dog for a while, and she often altered her voice sounding eerily like different members of the Bell family. Through it all, Betsy and John continued to receive the brunt of her most violent attacks.

Word spread throughout the state about the Bell Witch of Adams. Rumors about the ghost reached future U.S. President, Andrew Jackson. John Bell's boys, Jesse and John Jr., had fought alongside General Jackson in the famed Battle of New Orleans in 1812. Always curious and up for an adventure, Jackson called out to the Bell boys about the ghost. Still friendly acquaintances with the general, they invited him to visit and witness the phenomena himself. Jackson agreed and planned a trip from his home in Nashville to the countryside of Adams.

Several of Jackson's associates volunteered to travel with him. They packed a wagon led by four horses and the troupe began the journey to the Bell farm. For days they rode, growing more anxious about the trek's end and the mysteries that awaited them as they neared the destination. As Jackson's party reached the property line, the wagon quit moving.

"General!" one of the riders in the back called out, "We've got a problem back here."

Riding at the lead of the pack, Jackson turned around on his horse with a look of displeasure. "What's wrong back there? We're almost there."

"I think the wagon has a broken wheel," the rider answered back. As if on cue, the four horses all whined while they pulled unsuccessfully in front of the covered wagon.

"Damn," Jackson hissed and jumped down to the ground. The riders, and their horses between he and the wagon, all parted to make way as Jackson marched back to where the trouble was.

Jackson bent down to examine the wheels, but could not find any problem. Others joined him and they could also not find the cause.

One of the men spoke out, "Maybe this is the work of that Bell Witch."

In that instant, a high-pitched sigh was heard from somewhere in the trees. It was followed by a gravelly woman's voice. "*I've been waiting for you, General. I'll let you through, but know this; I will see you again tonight.*"

The moment the voice was gone, the wagon lurched forward scaring the men out of their wits. Jackson realized this was not just someone's imagination, but true evil at work.

They all spent the night at the farm, and John and Lucy Bell were honored to have the legendary General Jackson at their home. They fed the road-weary travelers, and after dinner they began to share some of their countless stories with the Witch. One of Jackson's cohorts stood up at the end of one of the tales and pulled a gun from beside him.

"Bring out that witch. I'll put her down like a rabid dog," he boasted mimicking the action of firing his rifle, "I'm the witch tamer. I'll put her in her place."

Jackson and his men laughed heartily at their bold, if not somewhat foolish, companion. The Bells looked on not quite so amused. They knew that somewhere the witch was listening.

"Ow," the 'witch tamer' said throwing his hand at his back. Some of the men continued laughing, thinking this was still part of his entertainment.

"Hey, now! Stop! Stop! It..," the man twisted and convulsed, while he grabbed with his arms at his back. He spun around twice and nearly fell. It was like watching someone being stung by hornets. He jumped and screamed as the intensity of the pain got worse. No one was laughing anymore. He started to run, but tripped on his own feet. His body was sprawled out on the ground and he continued to roll howling in pain.

No one dared to step near him, but everyone rose to their feet waiting for what else might come. The 'witch tamer' sat up looking all around him and frantically over each shoulder.

"What happened to you?" Jackson asked.

"I don't know. It was like someone was sticking me with a thousand pins," he said still looking around nervously for his invisible attacker. The familiar hoarse laugh of the Bell Witch filled their ears.

*"I'm not finished. No, not yet. There's one more imposter in your group, and I'll take care of him tomorrow night."*

They were unsure who that imposter was, and by the time the sun rose the next morning they had decided to pack up and leave. No one in the party wanted to find out if it was them. In later years, Jackson would famously speak of his experience, saying, "I'd rather face the entire British army than to spend one more night with the Bell Witch."

By 1820, the witch was still as active in their lives as ever. Even as the children grew and moved off of the farm, starting their own families, the inexorable witch followed them continuing her cruel haunts of the children. At the age of fourteen, Betsy Bell became engaged to a man named Joshua Gardner. Stories are that she was deeply in love with him and she looked forward to their marriage. It seems that Kate did not approve of the couple.

She visited Betsy one evening and warned:

*"I will not see you marry that man. I'm warning you now to end this with him, Betsy. If you don't, your life will become even more tortured than ever."*

"No!" Betsy barked defiantly, "I love him. Why shouldn't I marry him? You have been beating and hurting me since I was a little girl. It can't be any more awful than it is now, and I won't let you tell me what to do anymore!"

A moment passed. It was rare for Betsy to defy the malicious witch. Finally, the cruel voice said:

*"We shall see, young one. We shall see."*

Betsy felt a rare moment of triumph. The witch had ruled their lives for long enough, forcing them to live in fear. It was time for them to take control. Things couldn't be worse, she thought. Of course, she was wrong.

John Bell developed a nervous disorder involving ticks and seizures. In 1820, he became bedridden in their log cabin home. This didn't stop the witch from continuing her "visits." Even in the midst of the seizures, she would slap and claw at him, and the whole time she would laugh at her defenseless victim.

On December 20, 1820, Lucy entered the bedroom to check on John. His eyes were open, but lifeless, staring at the ceiling in a frozen expression of fear. Lucy ran to him and grabbed him on each side of his face with her hands. "John! John, my darling, wake up, wake up. Please, John. *Please.*"

She felt his chest and then his pulse at the wrist. Nothing. John was dead. Lucy fell in a heap on top of her beloved and sobbed. After some time, through her tears, Lucy saw an overturned vial on the nightstand. She reached for the unmarked container and held it in her hand. Behind her, Betsy and a few of the other children had appeared in the doorway, hearing their mother's cries. Their eyes were filling with tears, and Betsy's lip was quivering as she struggled to contain herself. The vial dropped from Lucy's hand as she rushed over to her children to comfort them.

Distantly, the family heard the familiar, raspy laugh of their ghost, Kate.

*"I told you I'd see you dead, John Bell. I poisoned him whilst he lied helpless on his bed."*

Their eyes all dropped to the vial on the floor, its contents being lapped up by the family cat. Lucy pulled the cat away and ushered him out the door. Together the family sobbed and mourned over John's body. They later noticed their pet dead in the hallway, apparently due to the vial of poison. John, Jr. picked up the vial and threw it into the fireplace were it broke into tiny pieces.

At the funeral, the witch made her presence known again. Kate's voice taunted the mourners. Applause, laughter, and singing could be heard from the witch throughout the ceremony. Even in death, John was not allowed dignity. Feelings of helplessness had become commonplace to the Bell family, but even more so during the funeral.

Realizing the deadly potential of Kate, Betsy tragically decided to break off her engagement with Joshua Gardner. To Joshua's credit, he begged Betsy not to leave him. He said he could endure the best the witch could offer, but the heartbroken Betsy Bell just shook her head. How could she allow the man she loved to face the brutality of Kate? She couldn't. Her love for him simply would not allow it. Together they cried and argued for hours. Joshua begged, but Betsy wouldn't budge.

The Bell Witch left the family in April of 1821, but she promised to return in seven years. The family was relieved when the cursed spirit was gone, but dreaded the day she would return. Betsy later married another man, a teacher named Richard Powell. Betsy had eight children, but four of them died before reaching adulthood. Occasionally, Betsy would be in town and would see Joshua Gardner. Briefly they'd make eye contact before she would turn her head and move away. She stayed faithfully married to her husband, but privately she often wondered what might have been if the witch had never entered her life.

In 1828, the Witch revisited the Bell family for a few weeks. During that time, she made a variety of predictions including premonitions involving the Civil War and other historic milestones. Before she left the second time, she said that she would revisit the Bell descendents 107 years later. Whether or not she returned is still a mystery. It's interesting to note however, that in 1935, the year the witch said she would return, several of the descendants of John Bell died of various causes.

Years later *The Saturday Night Evening Post* ran a story on the Bell Witch, which brought the phenomenon to the national spotlight. Ever since, interest in the Bell Witch has grown. Countless books, articles, investigations, documentaries, and even the film industry have revisited the horror that was the curse of the Bell clan.

The people of Adams, Tennessee do not all necessarily embrace the ghost stories. When asked about her, many will disingenuously claim to have not ever heard of the story. Some will not speak of her by name, fearing that they might bring her wrath upon them. For many, it's for religious reasons that they do not acknowledge her. Superstitions and myths of all kind have circulated about the Bell Witch all over the state.

Today, the log cabin is long gone, but below the site of the original farm, there is a cave that many believe is where the witch has retreated, due to a variety of bizarre events surrounding it in the years since. The sounds of dragging chains, screams, sightings of a woman with dark hair and fiery balls of light are just a few of the reports by witnesses in the last few decades.

The Bell Witch Cave is interesting in and of itself. An ancient grave of a Native American has been discovered there. Some think that he was a mystical medicine man and he is the source of the haunting. On one wall, there is a rock formation that appears to resemble a witch's face, which has gained a lot of attention from the curious. Perhaps it's true...that the witch has retreated deep into the dark recesses of that cavern, lying dormant these many years. Maybe the Bell Witch is sleeping there today.

Or maybe she's waiting.

Frankie Harris captivates audiences on the original Nashville Ghost Tour.

# Bibliography

Andrews, James. "The Ghost of St. Mary's." *Commonwealth Appeal Mid-South Magazine,* 25 November 1973.

Beard, W. E. *It Happened in Nashville, Tennessee.* Nashville, Tennessee: Mini-Histories, 1991.

Beard, William E. *Nashville: The Home of History Makers.* Nashville, Tennessee: Nashville Civitan Club, 1993.

Betts, Ann. "Area Has Share of Haunted Houses." *The Tennessean,* 31 October 1984.

Brown, Alan. *Haunted Places in the American South.* Jackson, Mississippi: University Press of Mississippi, 2002.

Burt, Jesse C. *Nashville: Its Life and Times.* Nashville, Tennessee: Tennessee Book Company, 1959.

Carey, Bill. *Fortunes, Fiddles, and Fried Chicken.* Franklin, Tennessee: Hillsboro Press, 2000.

Coleman, Christopher K. *Strange Tales of the Dark and Bloody Ground.* Nashville, Tennessee: Rutledge Hill Press, 1998.

Ewing, James. *A Treasury of Tennessee Tales.* Nashville, Tennessee: Rutledge Hill Press, 1997.

Hauck, Dennis William. *Haunted Places: The National Directory.* United States of America: Penguin Books, 2002.

Highland, Deborah. "Local Legends and Halloween Lore." *The Tennessean,* 30 October, 1996.

Kaczmarek, Dale. *National Register of Haunted Places.* Ghost Research Society, POB 205, Oaklawn, IL 60454. (Pamphlet.)

Kerr, Gail. "Workers at Ryman Tell of Spooky Moments." *The Tennessean,* 19 October, 2003.

Kingsbury, Paul. *The Grand Ole Opry: History of Country Music.* United States: Villard Books, 1995.

Lacey, T. Jensen. *Amazing Tennessee.* Nashville, Tennessee: Rutledge Hill Press, 2004.

McDaniel, Karina. *Nashville Then and Now.* San Diego, California: Thunder Bay Press, 2005.

Monroe, James. "Who's Who? Among Local Ghosts." *The Monocle,* 4 October 1988.

Mott, A.S. *Ghost Stories of Tennessee.* Canada: Lone Line Publishing, 2005

Zimmerman, Mark. *Guide to Civil War Nashville.* Nashville, Tennessee: Battle of Nashville Preservation Society, 2004.

# Index

Acklen, Adelicia, 77-90
Acklen, Joseph, 77, 81, 86
Adams, Tennessee, 6, 158, 164, 170
Akeman, Stringbean, 65
"America's Most Wanted," 135
Anderson, "Whispering" Bill, 61-62

Baxter, Mary, 10-16
Battle of New Orleans, 166
Battle of Nashville, 102, 111
Batts, Kate, 158, 165, 169
Bell, Betsy, 160, 163, 165–166, 168-170
Bell, John, 158-169
Bell, Lucy, 161,163-165, 167
Bell Witch, the, 6, 158-171
Bell Witch Cave, the, 171
Belmont Mansion, 78-82, 84, 86
Belmont University, 82-84, 88
Bess, Tootsie, 66-69
Black Bottoms District, 55
Bolanger, Robert, 109-110
Bottoms, Wayne, 109-110, 114-117
Breeze Hill, 102-104, 111, 118
Buffalo Billiards, 97

Carmack, Edward Ward, 91-96
Cashin, Father, 43, 49
Capitol Grille, 29
Capone, Al, 29,121, 130
Carmen, 56
Caveye, James, 135
Cline, Patsy, 53,62,65,68
Civil War, 21, 40, 44, 48, 81, 62-64, 102, 111, 145, 170
Concordia Society Club, 137
Confederate Gallery, 64
Confederacy, 8, 40, 44, 62, 64, 81-82, 97, 102, 145
Cooper, Col. Duncan, 93-96

Cooper, Robin, 93-96
Copas, Cowboy, 65
Cowan, Mildred, 116,118
Crossroads, 145
Cumberland River, 148

Dickinson, James McGavock, 23
Dorris, Mary, 10-16
Duffy, Father, 41-43

Edmondson, Georgia, 142-144
Ernest Tubb Record Shop, 145-147

Fats, Minnesota, 29,31
Fort Andrew Johnson, 21
Fox, "Texas Ruby," 65
Franklin, Isaac, 77

Gardner, Joshua, 168-170
Gospel Tabernacle, 56
Grand Ole Opry, the, 53, 58, 64, 130, 147
Gunn, Reverend, 164-166

'Hail to the Chief,' 25
Hayes, Randy, 65
Hawkins, John, 73-76
Hawkins, Hawkshaw, 65
"Hee Haw," 131, 133-134
Hermitage, the, 7-8, 10, 28-29
Hermitage Hotel, 29-38
Hines, Nell, 39, 41-42
Historic Belmont Auxiliary, 88
Hume-Fogg, 148-151

Jackson, Andrew, 8-10, 14-15, 25, 28-29, 158, 166-167
Jackson, Rachel, 8, 14, 25-28
Jackson, Uncle Alfred, 10-11, 14-15

James gang, the, 56
Johnston, James, 164
Jones, Sam, 54-56

Kristofferson, Kris, 68
Keenan, Charlie, 142-144

Ladies Hermitage Association, 9
Lewis, Major Eugene, 119
Lynn, Loretta, 53, 147

Mansfield, Mrs. J. R., 70-73, 75-76
Men's District, the, 130
Merchant's, 142-144
Midnight Jamboree, the, 147
Miles, Bishop Richard Pius, 45-46,
    48-49
Mom's Place, 66
Morgan, Monsignor, 43-44
Morgan, Samuel, 18-21
Mulligan's, 50-52

Nashville City Cemetery, 44
Nelson, Willie, 68

Opry curse, 64-65
Opryland, 65

Past Perfect, 152-157
Patterson, Malcolm, 91, 93, 95-96
Pearl, Minnie, 82
Polk, James K., 23-25, 93
Polk, Sarah Childress, 23-25
Polk Place, 23
Pride, Charlie, 68
Printer's Alley, 128-131

Rainbow Room, the, 130, 133-136
Reeves, Jim, 65
Red River Baptist Church, 158
Ryman Auditorium, 7, 53-66
Ryman, Capt. Tom, 54-58

Savage, Dr. Giles C., 137, 141
Savage House, 137
Scribner, Elizabeth, 104-110, 118
Scribner, William, 104-109, 118
Shore, Dinah, 29, 148
Shullman, Skull, 131-136
Southern Turf, the, 130-132
Spence, Jason, 135
St. Mary of the Seven Sorrows,
    39-49
Standard, the, 137
Strickland, Francis, 18
Strickland, William, 17-21, 23, 39

Tennessee State Capitol, 7, 17,
    19-23, 28, 29, 39
The Jimmy Dean Show, 57
Tobacco Road, 56
Tootsie's Orchid Lounge, 58,
    66-69

Union Gospel Tabernacle, 56, 64
Union Station, 119-127

Vaulx, Joseph, 102-104

Walker, John, 42
War Memorial Plaza, 17
Widener, Jimmy, 65
Williams Jr., Hank, 65
Williams Sr., Hank, 53, 58-62, 66,
    147
Wilson, Morris, 104
Women's Suffrage, 29
Wynette, Tammy, 135

York, Sgt. Alvin, 30